THE
BLOCKCHAIN REVOLUTION

BUILDING THE DIGITAL WORLD

Please check out this other great title

SIMPLE INVESTING TO MILLIONS
EVERYTHING I WISH I KNEW SOONER

- ✓ **Beginner Friendly** – You don't need to be an expert to understand this book.
- ✓ **Simple Steps** – It's written without complex jargon and focuses on the steps to make your $$$ work.
- ✓ **Money** – You can begin investing with your lunch money. Learn how to invest small amounts to compound into big savings!

This book can and WILL change your life and leave a lasting legacy for your family!

Copyright © 2024 Brian A. Kilheffer

All Rights Reserved

ISBN: 9798303616813

No part of this publication may be reproduced, distributed, or transmitted in any form or by any means, including photocopying, recording, or other electronic or mechanical methods, without the prior written permission of the author, except in the case of brief quotations embodied in reviews and certain other noncommercial uses permitted by copyright law.

Disclaimer: This book is designed to provide information in regard to the subject matter covered. The information provided in this book is for educational purposes only. The author does not offer advisory or brokerage services, nor does the author recommend or advise investors to buy or sell particular stocks, securities, or other investments. By its sale, neither the publisher nor the author is engaged in rendering financial advice or other financial professional services. The information contained in this book is not a substitute for financial advice from a professional who is aware of the facts and circumstances of your individual situation. If expert assistance, advice, or counseling is needed, the services of a competent professional should be sought. Past performance is no guarantee of future results.

Dear Valued Reader

Thank you so much! If you are satisfied with my work and writing, please consider leaving *positive* feedback. This book was personally written and designed by me and my family, and we would be thrilled if you could leave a review — it would mean so much to us and truly helps! ♡

If there is an issue with your order, please contact us first so we can resolve it before leaving feedback.

amazon.com/feedback

Table of Contents

Introduction 11
    Who This Book is For? 13

Part 1: Foundations of Blockchain Technology 19
    Chapter 1: What is Blockchain? 21
    Chapter 2: Origins and Evolution 29
    Chapter 3: How Blockchain Has Evolved 39

Part 2: Blockchain in Governance 49
    Chapter 4: Governments and Blockchain 51
    Chapter 5: Blockchain for Public Services 61

Part 3: Blockchain's Role in the Global Economy 71
    Chapter 6: Cryptocurrency Beyond Bitcoin 73
    Chapter 7: Blockchain for Business, Trade, and Finance 83

Part 4: Modern Applications of Blockchain Technology 89
    Chapter 8: Emerging Use Cases 91
    Chapter 9: Blockchain in Web3 99
    Chapter 10: Social Good and Sustainability 107
    Chapter 11: Artificial Intelligence and Combating Misinformation 115

Part 5: Challenges and Future Directions 123
    Chapter 12: Ongoing Concerns 125
    Chapter 13: Innovations on the Horizon 133
    Chapter 14: The Future of Blockchain 139

Conclusion 147
Blockchain's Next Chapter 149

Glossary 155

Key Takeaways 163

More Reading and Learning 171

More References and Sources 177

Introduction

Who This Book is For?

The world is on the cusp of monumental change, driven by what are often called **exponential technologies** — innovations that grow and improve at an accelerating pace, reshaping industries, economies, and lives in profound ways. Blockchain is one of these transformative technologies, offering the potential to redefine trust, transparency, and collaboration across a wide range of applications. This book is designed to guide readers through its complexities and opportunities, providing both foundational knowledge and forward-looking insights.

Whether you're a curious individual, a tech enthusiast, or a business leader, this book will help you understand blockchain's role in a rapidly evolving digital landscape and empower you to navigate its growing influence. It is not just a guide to blockchain's current capabilities but a lens into its future potential, encouraging everyone to explore how this technology might impact their personal and professional lives.

Understanding Exponential Technologies

Exponential technologies are advancements that develop at a rate far beyond traditional linear growth. These innovations often start small but grow rapidly, disrupting industries and creating entirely new paradigms. Key examples include:

1. **Artificial Intelligence (AI)**:
    - Machines capable of learning, reasoning, and making decisions.
    - Applications: Automation, predictive analytics, and deep fakes.
2. **Internet of Things (IoT)**:
    - Networks of connected devices that communicate and share data.
    - Applications: Smart homes, connected vehicles, and industrial automation.
3. **Augmented Reality (AR) and Virtual Reality (VR)**:
    - Technologies that blend the digital and physical worlds.
    - Applications: Gaming, education, and immersive experiences.

4. **Quantum Computing**:
    - Machines that process information at speeds unimaginable with classical computers.
    - Applications: Cryptography, drug discovery, and complex simulations.

5. **Biotechnology**:
    - Advances in genetic engineering, synthetic biology, and personalized medicine.
    - Applications: Gene editing, vaccine development, and bio-manufacturing.

6. **Blockchain**:
    - Decentralized, transparent, and secure systems for recording transactions and data.
    - Applications: Cryptocurrencies, supply chain management, digital identities, and more.

Among these, **blockchain stands out as the technology poised to underpin many others**, offering a framework for trust, security, and transparency in a digital-first world.

Why Blockchain is Essential

As a foundational layer for the future of technology, blockchain enables secure and immutable systems, bridging gaps in trust across industries and applications. Whether facilitating fair trade, combating misinformation, or enabling decentralized finance, blockchain has implications that extend far beyond cryptocurrencies.

Here's why blockchain deserves your attention:

- **Ubiquity**: Blockchain is finding applications in finance, healthcare, governance, and beyond.
- **Interoperability**: Blockchain can integrate with AI, IoT, and AR/VR to create seamless and trustworthy ecosystems. That's just the start…
- **Impact**: It has the potential to democratize access to resources, secure personal data, and create more equitable systems globally.

This book delves into these transformative possibilities, making blockchain accessible to all.

Who Will Benefit from This Book?

1. **Beginners and Curious Individuals**:
    - If you've heard of blockchain but feel overwhelmed by the jargon, this book will break down complex concepts into simple, relatable ideas.
    - Learn what blockchain is, how it works, and why it matters.
2. **Business Leaders and Entrepreneurs**:
    - Discover how blockchain can transform your industry and create new opportunities.

- Case studies and real-world examples will inspire you to innovate and adapt.

3. **Technologists and Innovators**:
    - Dive into blockchain's technical aspects, including smart contracts, consensus mechanisms, and integration with other exponential technologies.

4. **Students and Lifelong Learners**:
    - Understand blockchain's role in shaping the future of economies, governance, and global systems.
    - Build foundational knowledge to stay ahead in the digital economy.

5. **Policy Makers and Advocates**:
    - Explore how blockchain can be used to create fairer, more transparent systems for governance and public services.

A World of Change

Blockchain is no longer just a buzzword — it's an essential tool for navigating a world increasingly driven by digital systems. As it converges with other exponential technologies, its potential to create trust, enable efficiency, and foster innovation is limitless.

This book invites you to explore blockchain's transformative power, whether you're looking to understand its basics or envision its role in the future of technology. Together, we will uncover how blockchain is reshaping the world, one block at a time.

Part 1: Foundations of Blockchain Technology

Chapter 1: What is Blockchain?

Blockchain is often described as a revolutionary technology, but to fully appreciate its transformative potential, it's essential to understand what blockchain is and how it works. This chapter provides a detailed explanation of blockchain, its key features, and why it is uniquely positioned to address challenges in our increasingly digital world.

Simplified Explanation

At its core, blockchain is a digital ledger—a secure and tamper-proof record of transactions—that is maintained across a distributed network of computers. Unlike traditional databases, which are centralized and managed by a single authority, blockchain is decentralized. This means no single entity owns or controls it, and the ledger is collectively maintained by all participants, or **nodes**, in the network.

- **Immutable Records**: Once a transaction is added to the blockchain, it cannot be altered or deleted. This ensures a permanent, trustworthy record.
- **The "Block" in Blockchain**: Transactions or data are grouped into blocks, each containing:
    - The data itself (e.g., financial transactions, contracts).
    - A timestamp, ensuring chronological order.
    - A unique cryptographic hash that links it to the previous block.

The result is a chain of blocks, forming a transparent and secure record that is highly resistant to tampering.

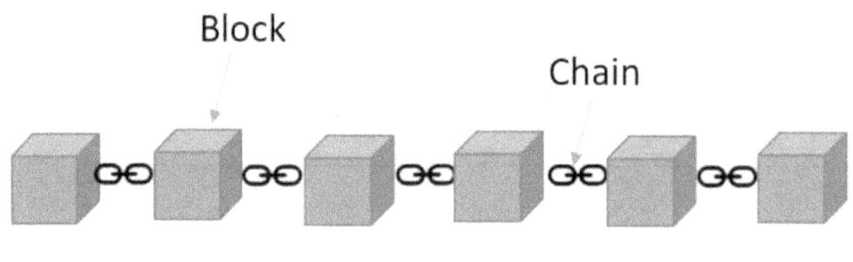

Blockchain

Here is an analogy: Think of blockchain as a digital version of a notebook that records every event or transaction. Everyone has a copy of the notebook, and any changes are instantly reflected in all copies. Since everyone has the same version, tampering with one copy is impossible without altering every other copy.

Key Features of Blockchain

Blockchain's transformative power lies in its unique design. Its decentralized structure, transparency, and security distinguish it from traditional systems.

Decentralization

Traditional systems, such as banks, rely on a central authority to manage and validate transactions. This creates a single point of failure—if the central system is compromised, the entire network can be disrupted. Blockchain eliminates this reliance by distributing the ledger across a network of participants, or nodes.

- **How It Works**: Each node in the blockchain network holds a complete copy of the ledger. When a new transaction is made, it is broadcast to all nodes. These nodes work together to validate the transaction through a consensus mechanism, ensuring accuracy and security.

- **Advantages**:
    - **Resilience**: The decentralized nature of blockchain ensures there is no single point of failure.
    - **Redundancy**: Even if some nodes fail, the system remains operational because the ledger is stored across the network.

Example: In cryptocurrency networks like Bitcoin, decentralization allows users to transfer funds without needing a bank or intermediary, reducing costs and increasing efficiency.

Transparency

Blockchain's design makes all transactions visible to participants in the network, fostering trust and accountability. This transparency is especially valuable in systems where trust is critical.

- **How It Works**: Each transaction is recorded on the blockchain and linked to the previous block, creating a public record accessible to all participants. While personal information remains private, the transaction data itself is open for verification.
- **Advantages**:
    - **Accountability**: Participants can independently verify the validity of transactions.
    - **Auditability**: The blockchain's chronological structure provides a complete history of all activities.

Use Case: In supply chain management, blockchain enables stakeholders to track a product's journey from origin to destination. For example, a coffee retailer can verify that beans were ethically sourced and transported under proper conditions.

Security

Blockchain is designed to be inherently secure, using advanced cryptographic methods to protect data. Its decentralized and consensus-based nature makes it resistant to tampering and fraud.

- **How It Works**:
    - Each block is linked to the previous one using a cryptographic hash.
    - Any attempt to alter a block would require changing all subsequent blocks across every node in the network, which is computationally infeasible.
    - Transactions are validated by the network through consensus mechanisms like **Proof-of-Work (PoW)** or **Proof-of-Stake (PoS)**.[1]

- **Advantages**:
    - **Integrity**: Data cannot be altered once it is added to the blockchain.

---

[1] Proof-of-Work (PoW) is a consensus mechanism that requires network participants, known as miners, to solve complex mathematical problems to validate transactions and create new blocks. This process is computationally intensive and energy-demanding but ensures security and decentralization. Proof-of-Stake (PoS), on the other hand, selects validators based on the amount of cryptocurrency they hold and are willing to "stake" as collateral. PoS is more energy-efficient than PoW and reduces the environmental impact of blockchain networks while maintaining security.

- **Resistance to Hacks**: A successful attack would require control of more than 50% of the network, an exceedingly difficult task in large networks.

Example: In financial transactions, blockchain secures data from unauthorized access, reducing risks of fraud and identity theft.

Applications of Blockchain

While this chapter focuses on blockchain's fundamentals, its features make it suitable for a wide range of applications:

- **Cryptocurrencies**: Blockchain underpins digital currencies like Bitcoin and Ethereum, enabling secure peer-to-peer transactions without intermediaries.
- **Healthcare**: Protects patient data while enabling secure and seamless sharing between providers.
- **Voting Systems**: Creates tamper-proof digital ballots, enhancing transparency and trust in elections.
- **Intellectual Property**: Provides a secure record of ownership, preventing unauthorized use or duplication.

Debunking Common Myths

Understanding what blockchain is also involves clarifying what it is not:

- **Myth**: Blockchain is only for cryptocurrencies.
  - **Fact**: Blockchain has diverse applications, from supply chain management to identity verification.

- **Myth**: Blockchain is completely anonymous.
    - **Fact**: While blockchain ensures privacy, transactions can often be traced back to participants using public keys.
- **Myth**: Blockchain is tamper-proof.
    - **Fact**: While blockchain is highly secure, vulnerabilities can arise from poorly implemented systems or external factors, such as compromised private keys.

In summary, what is blockchain:

Blockchain is a groundbreaking technology that transforms how data is stored, shared, and secured. Its **decentralized**, **transparent**, and **secure** design addresses challenges in trust, efficiency, and fraud, making it a cornerstone of the digital age.

As we move to the next chapter, we will explore how blockchain has evolved beyond its original purpose, becoming a transformative force in industries worldwide.

Chapter 2: Origins and Evolution

The Origins of Blockchain Technology

Before 2008, digital transactions relied heavily on centralized systems, such as banks or payment platforms, to mediate and validate exchanges of value. While effective, these systems came with inherent drawbacks, including high fees, potential for fraud, and vulnerability to hacking. The search for a decentralized solution — a system that could operate without the need for trusted intermediaries — had long been a goal of cryptographers and computer scientists. The concept of a secure, tamper-proof digital ledger had been explored, but a practical implementation remained elusive. This changed with the advent of blockchain technology.

Blockchain technology was introduced in 2008 with the release of Bitcoin, described in a whitepaper titled **"Bitcoin: A Peer-to-Peer Electronic Cash System"** by an anonymous figure or group under the pseudonym **Satoshi Nakamoto**.[2] The paper outlined a revolutionary approach to transferring value online without relying on centralized intermediaries like banks or payment processors.

At its core, blockchain solved the problem of **double-spending**, ensuring that digital currency (Bitcoin) could not be copied or spent more than once. This was achieved by introducing a **distributed ledger** technology, which recorded transactions transparently and immutably across a decentralized network of computers. Key features included:

- **Decentralization**: No single entity controlled the system. Instead, all participants collectively maintained the ledger.

- **Transparency**: All transaction records were visible to participants, enhancing trust.

- **Immutability**: Once a transaction was added to the blockchain, it could not be altered or removed.

The first-ever Bitcoin transaction occurred on January 12, 2009, between Nakamoto and Hal Finney, a renowned cryptographer. This marked the beginning of a decentralized financial revolution.

---

[2] Satoshi Nakamoto is the pseudonym used by the unknown creator (or creators) of Bitcoin and its underlying blockchain technology. Despite extensive speculation and investigation, Nakamoto's true identity remains a mystery. Their work introduced the concept of decentralized digital currencies and set the foundation for modern blockchain technology.

How Blockchain Works

A blockchain is a type of distributed database that stores information digitally and is shared across nodes in a computer network. Unlike traditional databases, which organize data into tables, a blockchain structures data into blocks. These blocks are linked together in a chain, forming a shared, immutable ledger. Once a block is filled with data, it is connected to the previous block in the chain. While a blockchain can store various types of information, its primary use is for recording transactions.

Understanding blockchain's functionality is crucial to appreciating its transformative impact:

1. **Blocks**: Blockchain records data in groups called blocks. Each block contains transaction data, a timestamp, and a cryptographic hash of the previous block.

2. **The Chain**: Blocks are linked in chronological order, forming a chain. This structure ensures the integrity of the entire ledger.

3. **Consensus Mechanisms**: Transactions are validated through consensus algorithms like **Proof-of-Work (PoW)**, where participants solve complex mathematical problems to add blocks to the chain.

4. **Distributed Nature**: A copy of the blockchain ledger is stored on multiple computers (nodes), ensuring redundancy and security.

This design eliminated the need for intermediaries, enabling direct transactions between parties, which became the foundation for Bitcoin and other cryptocurrencies.

Here is a visual representation of how blockchains work:

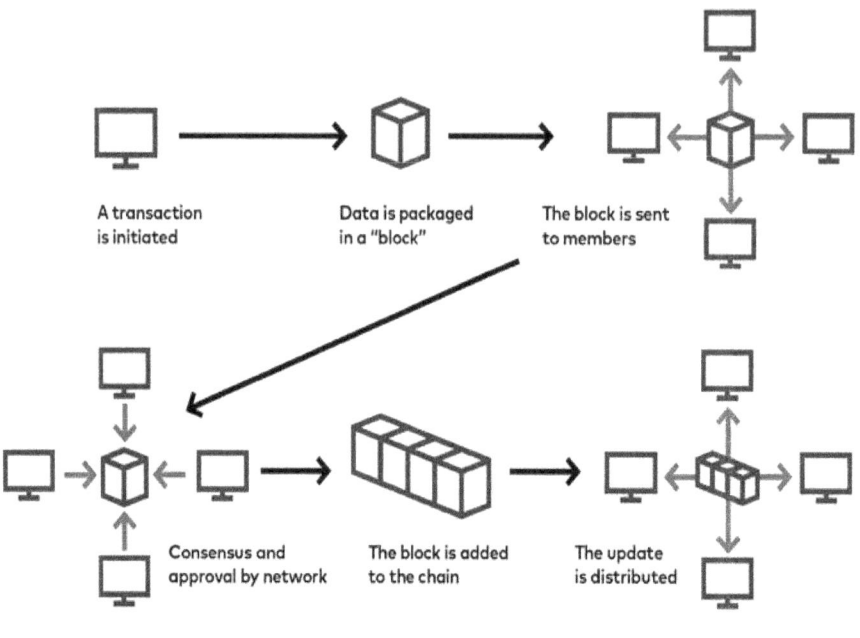

Evolution Beyond Cryptocurrencies

Blockchain's applications have grown far beyond its origins as the backbone of Bitcoin. Innovators recognized its potential to disrupt industries, leading to groundbreaking advancements:

- **Smart Contracts**:
  In 2015, **Ethereum**, a blockchain platform created by Vitalik Buterin, introduced **smart contracts** — programmable agreements that automatically execute when specific conditions are met. These contracts eliminated the need for intermediaries in legal, financial, and business

agreements, unlocking new possibilities for automation and trust.

- **Non-Fungible Tokens (NFTs)**:
  Blockchain enabled the creation of unique digital assets known as **NFTs**, which proved ownership and authenticity. NFTs revolutionized:
    - **Digital Art**: Artists could sell their work directly to buyers while retaining royalties for future sales.
    - **Gaming**: Players owned and traded in-game items as NFTs, introducing real-world value to virtual economies.

- **Decentralized Finance (DeFi)**:
  DeFi platforms disrupted traditional banking by enabling:
    - Peer-to-peer lending and borrowing.
    - Decentralized trading on blockchain-based exchanges.
    - Transparent financial instruments without centralized oversight.

These innovations demonstrated blockchain's ability to foster trust, transparency, and efficiency in sectors far removed from its cryptocurrency roots.

The Rise of Public and Private Blockchains

As blockchain technology matured, different types of blockchains emerged to suit various use cases:

- **Public Blockchains**:
  Open to anyone, public blockchains like Bitcoin and Ethereum are decentralized and transparent, ensuring trust and security through community participation.

- **Private Blockchains**:
  Restricted to specific participants, private blockchains offer enhanced control and efficiency for enterprises while sacrificing some decentralization. They are widely used in supply chain management and finance.

- **Consortium Blockchains**:
  A hybrid approach where multiple organizations manage a blockchain collaboratively, striking a balance between decentralization and control.

These variations allowed blockchain to expand its reach and address diverse challenges across industries.

Blockchain's Role in Transforming Industries

Blockchain has found applications in numerous fields, revolutionizing how industries operate:

- **Healthcare**:
  Blockchain secures patient data, ensures privacy, and enables interoperability between healthcare providers. It also tracks pharmaceutical supply chains to prevent counterfeit drugs.

- **Supply Chain Management**:
  By providing real-time traceability of goods, blockchain

enhances transparency and reduces fraud. Companies like Walmart have adopted blockchain to improve food safety and logistics.

- **Governance**:
Blockchain is being used to create tamper-proof voting systems, manage public records, and ensure transparency in government operations.

- **Energy**:
Decentralized energy grids use blockchain to facilitate peer-to-peer energy trading, promoting renewable energy adoption.

These examples highlight blockchain's ability to address critical inefficiencies, promote transparency, and enhance security.

Blockchain Today and Tomorrow

Today, blockchain stands as one of the most transformative technologies of the 21st century. Its applications continue to grow, driven by advancements in scalability, integration with emerging technologies like AI and IoT, and the push for decentralized systems.

Future developments are expected to include:

- **Scalable Solutions**: Improved consensus mechanisms like Proof-of-Stake (PoS) and Layer 2 technologies are addressing blockchain's scalability challenges.

- **Mass Adoption**: Industries such as finance, healthcare, and logistics are poised for blockchain-driven transformations.

- **Global Collaboration**: Efforts to establish international standards and regulations are paving the way for widespread adoption.

Blockchain's potential to reshape economies, governance, and global systems is only beginning to be realized.

Chapter 3: How Blockchain Has Evolved

Blockchain technology has undergone remarkable evolution since its inception as the foundation of Bitcoin in 2008. What began as a mechanism for secure, peer-to-peer digital transactions has expanded into a transformative technology with applications spanning finance, art, governance, and beyond. This chapter explores the milestones in blockchain's journey, highlighting its progression from a niche innovation to a cornerstone of modern digital systems. From the introduction of smart contracts to the rise of decentralized finance (DeFi) and non-fungible tokens (NFTs), blockchain has consistently pushed the boundaries of innovation. Its continued evolution promises to reshape industries, redefine trust, and create new opportunities for collaboration and efficiency in a digital-first world.

The Early Days of Blockchain

In 2008, an anonymous entity known as **Satoshi Nakamoto** introduced Bitcoin, a decentralized digital currency, and its underlying blockchain technology. This marked the first successful implementation of a blockchain and addressed a critical challenge in digital transactions: trust.

The Problem of Trust:
Digital transactions traditionally required intermediaries, such as banks or payment processors, to verify and facilitate exchanges. These intermediaries added cost, delay, and risk of fraud. Blockchain eliminated the need for intermediaries by enabling:

- **Peer-to-peer transactions**: Direct exchanges between users without central authorities.

- **Decentralized verification**: Validation of transactions by a network of participants (nodes).

Bitcoin's Success:
Bitcoin's blockchain ensured transaction security and transparency through its distributed ledger. Transactions were grouped into blocks, secured via cryptographic hashing, and linked chronologically, forming an immutable chain.

- The first Bitcoin block, known as the **Genesis Block**, was mined on January 3, 2009, heralding a new era of decentralized finance.

While Bitcoin's blockchain showcased the power of decentralization and transparency, its initial focus was limited to financial transactions. This was just the beginning of blockchain's broader potential.

Beyond Bitcoin: Expanding Blockchain's Capabilities

As blockchain gained recognition, innovators began exploring its versatility. This led to groundbreaking developments that extended blockchain's utility beyond cryptocurrencies, including **smart contracts**, **non-fungible tokens (NFTs)**, and **decentralized finance (DeFi)**.

Smart Contracts: Automating Trust

In 2015, Ethereum introduced **smart contracts**, a pivotal innovation that transformed blockchain into a programmable platform.[3] Unlike Bitcoin, which primarily supported monetary transactions, Ethereum enabled developers to build applications on its blockchain.

- **What Are Smart Contracts?**
  Smart contracts are self-executing agreements encoded directly into a blockchain. They automatically enforce terms when predefined conditions are met, eliminating the need for intermediaries like lawyers or escrow services.

---

[3] Ethereum is a decentralized blockchain platform founded by Vitalik Buterin. It allows developers to build and deploy decentralized applications (DApps) using its native cryptocurrency, Ether (ETH), and smart contract functionality. Unlike Bitcoin, which focuses primarily on digital currency, Ethereum is designed as a flexible platform for executing programmable transactions and applications.

- **Applications of Smart Contracts**:
    - **Supply Chains**: Automating payments to suppliers upon delivery verification.
    - **Insurance**: Streamlining claims processing by triggering payouts when specific conditions, such as natural disasters, are met.
    - **Gaming and Entertainment**: Powering decentralized applications (DApps) for secure in-game asset transactions.
- **Impact**:
  Smart contracts revolutionized how agreements are executed, reducing costs, increasing efficiency, and minimizing the risk of disputes.

Non-Fungible Tokens (NFTs): Redefining Ownership

Blockchain also enabled the creation of **non-fungible tokens (NFTs)**, which represent unique digital assets. Unlike cryptocurrencies, which are interchangeable (fungible), NFTs are one-of-a-kind and linked to specific digital or physical items. This uniqueness allows NFTs to verify ownership and provenance, making them particularly valuable for digital art, collectibles, and virtual real estate. Their applications have extended into industries such as gaming, music, and even ticketing systems, revolutionizing how creators monetize and interact with their audiences.

- **Why NFTs Matter**:
  NFTs make it possible to verify ownership and authenticity

in the digital realm. Each NFT is stored on a blockchain, providing a transparent and tamper-proof record of provenance.[4]

- **Applications and Industries**:
    - **Digital Art**: NFTs allow artists to sell their work directly to buyers while retaining royalties for future sales.
    - **Gaming**: Players can own, trade, and monetize in-game items as NFTs.
    - **Virtual Real Estate**: Digital worlds like Decentraland and The Sandbox offer NFTs representing parcels of virtual land.

- **Broader Implications**:
    NFTs have bridged the gap between digital and physical ownership, creating new revenue streams for creators and industries. Beyond art and collectibles, they are now being used for virtual real estate, ticketing systems, and brand loyalty programs, further expanding their influence and utility across sectors.

---

[4] Provenance refers to the documented history of ownership and origin of an asset. In the context of NFTs, blockchain ensures that this history is immutable and publicly verifiable, providing confidence in the authenticity and rightful ownership of the digital or physical asset.

Decentralized Finance (DeFi): Reinventing Financial Systems

Blockchain's evolution into **decentralized finance (DeFi)** has disrupted traditional banking by enabling a new financial ecosystem. DeFi platforms operate without central authorities, giving users full control over their assets.

- **Core Features of DeFi**:
    - **Lending and Borrowing**: Peer-to-peer platforms enable users to lend or borrow assets directly.
    - **Decentralized Exchanges (DEXs)**: Allow trading of cryptocurrencies without intermediaries.
    - **Savings and Investments**: Yield-generating protocols offer alternatives to traditional banking products.
- **Benefits of DeFi**:
    - **Inclusion**: Extends financial services to unbanked populations worldwide.
    - **Transparency**: Every transaction is recorded on the blockchain, ensuring accountability.
    - **Cost Efficiency**: Reduces reliance on intermediaries, lowering fees.
- **Examples**:
  Platforms like Uniswap and Aave have gained widespread adoption, showcasing DeFi's potential to democratize finance.

The Rise of Blockchain Ecosystems

Blockchain's evolution is also characterized by the emergence of diverse ecosystems tailored to specific use cases:

- **Public Blockchains**: Open networks like Ethereum and Solana support decentralized applications and projects.

- **Private Blockchains**: Used by enterprises for internal operations, such as supply chain management or document verification.

- **Hybrid Blockchains**: Combining public and private elements to balance transparency with control.

These ecosystems highlight blockchain's adaptability, making it suitable for industries ranging from healthcare to logistics.

The versatility of these ecosystems has fueled widespread adoption, enabling businesses and developers to choose the framework that best suits their needs. This flexibility has not only driven innovation across industries but also fostered collaboration between public and private entities, paving the way for hybrid solutions that blend the strengths of both models.

From Technology to Transformation

Blockchain's evolution demonstrates its potential to redefine how we interact, transact, and govern in a digital-first world. The advancements in smart contracts, NFTs, and DeFi reflect just a fraction of its capabilities. As blockchain continues to evolve, its impact will likely extend further into artificial intelligence, IoT, and the metaverse, enabling innovations that are still unimaginable today.

From its beginnings as the technology behind Bitcoin, blockchain has grown into a multifaceted platform powering some of the most innovative solutions of the modern era. Each evolution — from enabling smart contracts to revolutionizing digital ownership with NFTs and creating a decentralized financial ecosystem with DeFi — has expanded blockchain's relevance and applications.

This journey illustrates blockchain's potential not just to disrupt existing systems but to enable entirely new possibilities. As we transition to the next chapter, focusing on blockchain's role in governance, we begin to explore how this technology is transforming public systems and institutions, paving the way for a more transparent and efficient world.

Part 2: Blockchain in Governance

Chapter 4: Governments and Blockchain

Blockchain technology is emerging as a transformative force in governance, with the potential to streamline operations, increase transparency, and enhance trust between governments and citizens. While its roots lie in powering digital currencies like Bitcoin, blockchain's decentralized and secure nature has prompted governments around the world to explore its use for public administration and service delivery. The secure and tamper-proof nature of blockchain makes it a plausible candidate for managing sensitive or classified data, such as secure communication, intelligence sharing, or supply chain verification in defense contexts. Some militaries and government agencies have expressed interest in blockchain's potential for secure and decentralized operations.

Adoption Trends

Governments face persistent challenges in managing data securely, transparently, and efficiently. Blockchain technology offers solutions to these challenges through its unique features: decentralization, immutability, and transparency. These features enable governments to streamline operations, reduce corruption, and foster public trust. By leveraging blockchains, governments can also enhance citizen engagement by providing verifiable, tamper-proof records and services, ultimately creating a more accountable and efficient governance framework.

Digital Identities

One of the most significant opportunities for blockchain lies in the management of **digital identities**. Current identity systems are often centralized, making them prone to breaches and fraud. Blockchain enables a decentralized approach to identity management by allowing citizens to control access to their personal data while ensuring its authenticity.

- **Advantages**:
  - Citizens can share only necessary information (e.g., proving age without revealing birthdate).
  - Governments reduce risks of identity theft and administrative errors.
  - Streamlined processes for issuing IDs, licenses, and passports.

Example: Estonia's e-Residency program provides global citizens with secure digital identities, enabling access to services like business registration and banking.

Land Registries

Traditional systems for managing property ownership often suffer from inefficiencies, corruption, and disputes. Blockchain can transform **land registries** by creating a single, immutable source of truth for property ownership and transactions.

How Blockchain Helps:

- Records are tamper-proof and instantly verifiable.
- Transactions are processed faster, reducing costs and delays.
- Blockchain minimizes opportunities for fraud by providing transparent transaction histories.

Example: Sweden's land registry uses blockchain to digitize and secure property transactions, simplifying the process for buyers, sellers, and government officials.

Public Records

From birth certificates to marriage licenses and tax records, **public records** are the backbone of government administration. Blockchain ensures these records are accurate, immutable, and easily accessible.

Benefits:
- Reduces reliance on vulnerable paper-based systems.
- Improves efficiency in record retrieval and verification.
- Enhances citizen trust by ensuring data integrity.

Example: Illinois has implemented blockchain for vital records like birth certificates and property titles, reducing administrative overhead and fraud.

Case Studies

To better understand how blockchain is transforming governance, let's explore several case studies from around the world. These examples illustrate the diverse ways governments are using blockchain to address challenges, enhance efficiency, and build trust with their citizens.

Illinois: Leading Blockchain Innovation

Illinois has pioneered the use of blockchain in public services, focusing on transparency and efficiency.

- **Birth Records and Property Titles**: Blockchain ensures secure and accessible records, eliminating fraudulent claims and administrative complexities.

- **Renewable Energy Credits**:
  By using blockchain to track renewable energy production, Illinois promotes accountability and sustainability.

Estonia: A Digital Governance Trailblazer

Estonia is often cited as a global leader in blockchain adoption, seamlessly integrating the technology into its digital governance framework.

- **e-Residency Program**:
  Offers a digital identity for global citizens, enabling them to open businesses and access government services remotely.
    - Citizens retain control over their data.
    - Businesses are empowered to operate internationally with reduced bureaucratic barriers.
- **Public Services**:
  Estonia secures sensitive government data and facilitates efficient communication between citizens and public offices.

Other Global Initiatives

Blockchain's versatility is demonstrated by its adoption across various governance systems worldwide:

- **Sweden**: Uses blockchain for land registries, simplifying property transactions and enhancing security.

- **Dubai**: Aims to become a fully blockchain-powered government by digitizing all documents and records, reducing paperwork and administrative costs.

- **India**: Pilots blockchain systems for welfare distribution to ensure funds reach intended recipients without leakage or fraud.

These examples illustrate blockchain's potential to address diverse challenges across different governance models.

Challenges in Adoption

While blockchain offers immense promise for governance, scaling its implementation across government systems is a complex undertaking. Governments face numerous obstacles that must be addressed to fully unlock the potential of blockchain in public administration. These challenges include navigating regulatory uncertainty, balancing transparency with privacy, and overcoming gaps in technology literacy.

Regulatory Hurdles

One of the primary challenges in adopting blockchain lies in the lack of consistent regulatory frameworks. Blockchain operates differently from traditional systems, and existing laws often struggle to accommodate its decentralized nature. For example, cross-border applications of blockchain face complications due to the absence of global standards, which leads to legal ambiguities and hinders international collaboration.

To overcome these hurdles, governments must work together to create cohesive regulations that address blockchain's unique characteristics. International cooperation is critical to establishing standards that allow blockchain to function seamlessly across jurisdictions. Some countries have adopted a **sandboxing approach**, where new blockchain applications are tested in controlled environments before being implemented at scale. This method provides a safe way to explore the technology's capabilities while minimizing risks.[5]

Transparency vs. Privacy

Blockchain's defining feature—transparency—can also be a double-edged sword. While public blockchains foster accountability by making all transactions visible, they can inadvertently expose sensitive personal or institutional data. This creates a tension between the need for public accountability and the responsibility to protect privacy.

Balancing these priorities requires careful design and the use of innovative solutions. **Permissioned blockchains**, for instance, restrict access to authorized participants, allowing governments to maintain transparency within specific boundaries. Similarly, advanced cryptographic techniques like **zero-knowledge proofs** enable data verification without revealing the underlying details.

---

[5] Risks include financial loss from poorly designed smart contracts, data breaches from misconfigured systems, scalability issues causing delays or increased costs, and regulatory non-compliance due to unclear legal frameworks.

These approaches ensure that blockchain systems can provide transparency without compromising the confidentiality of sensitive information.

Technology Literacy Gaps

The adoption of blockchain requires a deep understanding of its technical aspects, yet many government agencies lack the expertise needed to implement and manage this technology. Decision-makers often have limited knowledge of blockchain's potential, which can lead to resistance or ineffective deployment. Additionally, the absence of training for public sector employees further compounds the problem, leaving critical gaps in the skills needed to operate blockchain systems effectively.

Addressing these gaps requires a commitment to education and collaboration. Governments can partner with blockchain organizations and experts to share knowledge and provide guidance on best practices. Investing in training programs for government staff is equally important, as it ensures that employees are equipped to manage and maintain blockchain-based systems. By building technological capacity within public institutions, governments can pave the way for smoother adoption and more impactful results.

Navigating the Road Ahead

The challenges facing blockchain adoption in governance are significant, but they are not insurmountable. By establishing clear and supportive regulatory frameworks, designing systems that balance transparency and privacy, and investing in education and capacity-building, governments can overcome these barriers. Addressing these challenges is not just about enabling blockchain—it's about creating the foundation for more efficient, transparent, and inclusive governance systems that can meet the demands of the 21st century.

Blockchain technology is reshaping how governments operate by addressing inefficiencies, enhancing transparency, and building trust with citizens. Applications like digital identities, land registries, and public records showcase its potential to revolutionize public administration. Case studies from Illinois, Estonia, and other global initiatives demonstrate the transformative power of blockchain in governance.

However, to achieve widespread adoption, governments must address challenges like regulatory uncertainty, privacy concerns, and technology literacy gaps. By embracing blockchain, governments can provide faster, fairer, and more secure services, ensuring they are prepared to meet the demands of the 21st century.

Blockchain's integration into governance is not just a technological shift—it is a step toward more transparent, accountable, and citizen-focused systems. Let this be a guide to understanding how blockchain can empower governments and enhance the lives of citizens worldwide.

Chapter 5: Blockchain for Public Services

Public services are the backbone of a well-functioning society, but inefficiencies, fraud, and limited access often undermine their effectiveness. Blockchain technology offers innovative solutions to these challenges, enabling secure, transparent, and efficient systems for critical services such as voting and welfare distribution. By leveraging blockchain's unique attributes, governments and organizations can revolutionize how public services are delivered and trusted. Additionally, blockchain reduces administrative overhead by automating processes and eliminating intermediaries, ensuring resources are allocated more effectively. Its tamper-proof records also enhance accountability, fostering greater public trust in governmental operations. As adoption grows, blockchain has the potential to bridge gaps in service delivery, particularly for underserved and vulnerable populations.

Blockchain in Voting Systems

Voting is one of the cornerstones of democracy, yet many electoral systems today face significant challenges, including vulnerability to fraud, tampering, and diminishing public trust. Blockchain technology has emerged as a potential solution, offering a way to build tamper-proof and transparent voting mechanisms that could enhance the integrity of elections and restore confidence in democratic processes.

At the heart of blockchain's promise for voting is its decentralized and immutable nature. Traditional voting systems—whether paper-based or electronic—are often susceptible to interference. Centralized databases, for instance, can be hacked, and physical ballots can be tampered with. Blockchain addresses these vulnerabilities by recording votes on a distributed ledger that is not controlled by any single entity. Once a vote is added to the blockchain, it becomes a permanent, unalterable part of the record. This ensures that no individual or organization can manipulate the results after the fact.

Beyond its security features, blockchain brings a new level of transparency to elections. Every vote recorded on the blockchain is part of a public ledger that all stakeholders can access and verify. While voters' identities remain private, the system allows each person to confirm that their vote was counted correctly. This ability to independently verify election outcomes not only strengthens trust but also reduces disputes and accusations of fraud, fostering greater participation and belief in the democratic process.

Governments and organizations around the world are beginning to explore blockchain-based voting systems, with some notable successes. **Estonia**, a global leader in e-governance, has integrated blockchain into its remote voting infrastructure. Citizens can securely cast their votes from anywhere in the world, knowing that their participation is verified and their ballot is tamper-proof. Estonia's model demonstrates how blockchain can enable both security and convenience in elections.

In the United States, **West Virginia** made headlines in 2018 by piloting a blockchain voting system for overseas military personnel. This initiative provided secure and accessible voting options for individuals who might otherwise face logistical challenges in casting their ballots. The success of the program underscored blockchain's potential to extend voting rights to remote or underserved populations.

Similarly, **India** is exploring the use of blockchain to tackle one of its most persistent electoral challenges: enabling remote voting for migrant workers. By leveraging blockchain, the country hopes to ensure that millions of citizens who are unable to vote due to geographic or logistical barriers can still participate in the democratic process. If successful, this initiative could serve as a model for other nations seeking to make elections more inclusive.

These real-world examples illustrate blockchain's transformative potential for voting systems. By addressing long-standing issues of fraud and transparency, blockchain technology is paving the way for more secure, accessible, and trustworthy elections. As governments continue to pilot and refine these systems, the prospect of blockchain-powered voting becoming a global standard grows ever closer.

Blockchain in Welfare Programs

Governments face challenges in ensuring that welfare benefits and humanitarian aid reach their intended recipients without inefficiencies or corruption. Blockchain technology offers a secure and transparent solution, transforming welfare programs to maximize their impact.

Reducing Fraud and Increasing Efficiency

Blockchain's transparent nature ensures that every transaction is recorded and verifiable, minimizing opportunities for fraud. Removing intermediaries simplifies distribution and reduces costs, making aid delivery more efficient.

- **Transparency**: Blockchain's public ledger allows for real-time auditing of aid distribution, ensuring accountability.
- **Efficiency**: Automated smart contracts can trigger disbursements once predefined conditions, such as identity verification, are met.

Reaching Unbanked Populations

Many people in developing regions lack access to traditional banking systems, making aid distribution difficult. Blockchain enables direct welfare payments to individuals without requiring a bank account. Digital wallets can be linked to biometric authentication, ensuring secure and inclusive access to benefits.

- **Accessibility**: Recipients can receive aid through mobile devices or other digital platforms, bypassing traditional financial infrastructure.

- **Security**: Blockchain's cryptographic safeguards protect against identity theft and fraud.

Case Study: UN's Blockchain Program for Syrian Refugees

The United Nations World Food Program (WFP) implemented a blockchain-based system to provide cash transfers to Syrian refugees in Jordan. This initiative highlights blockchain's potential to improve humanitarian efforts:

- **Biometric Integration**: Refugees used eye-scanning technology to authenticate their identities and access funds through digital wallets.

- **Cost Savings**: By eliminating intermediaries such as banks, the program reduced administrative costs significantly.

- **Transparency and Accountability**: Blockchain provided a detailed and tamper-proof record of all transactions, ensuring that aid reached those who needed it most.

- **Local Impact**: Refugees used funds to purchase food locally, supporting the host community's economy.

This program set a benchmark for using blockchain in humanitarian aid and showcased its potential for future initiatives.

Transforming Public Services with Blockchain

The use of blockchain in voting and welfare programs showcases the immense potential of this technology to revolutionize public services. By addressing inefficiencies, enhancing transparency, and expanding access, blockchain enables governments to interact with and support their citizens in new and transformative ways.

One of the key benefits of blockchain in public services is its ability to promote **equity**. Marginalized populations often face barriers to accessing essential services, whether due to geographic isolation, lack of financial infrastructure, or systemic inefficiencies. Blockchain removes many of these barriers by creating systems that are inclusive by design. For example, direct aid distribution through blockchain eliminates the need for intermediaries, ensuring that resources reach the people who need them most.

Another significant advantage is **transparency**. Traditional systems often obscure the flow of funds and decisions, leading to inefficiencies and mistrust. Blockchain's immutable ledger provides a clear, tamper-proof record of every transaction and decision, allowing citizens to hold institutions accountable. This openness fosters greater trust between governments and their people, reinforcing the social contract.

Efficiency is another area where blockchain excels. Automating processes through smart contracts reduces administrative delays and costs, enabling governments to deliver services faster and with fewer resources. Whether it's disbursing welfare payments, processing votes, or managing public records, blockchain streamlines operations, freeing up resources for other priorities.

Looking ahead, the potential applications of blockchain in public services extend far beyond voting and welfare. For instance, in

healthcare, blockchain could securely store and share patient records, ensuring privacy while enabling seamless coordination among providers. This would improve outcomes and reduce redundancies in care.

In **education**, blockchain could play a critical role in verifying academic credentials and simplifying scholarship distribution. Students and employers alike could benefit from instant access to verified educational achievements, cutting down on administrative bottlenecks.

Even in **infrastructure**, blockchain offers transformative possibilities. Governments could use blockchain to track public funds, ensuring that budgets are spent as intended and eliminating corruption in development projects. Citizens, in turn, would gain greater confidence in the accountability of public initiatives.

These examples highlight just a few of the ways blockchain could reshape public services, creating systems that are more equitable, transparent, and efficient. By embracing this technology, governments can not only address longstanding challenges but also build a foundation for more trustworthy and responsive institutions in the digital age.

Harnessing Blockchain for Public Services

Blockchain offers governments and organizations an unprecedented opportunity to improve public services. In voting systems, it enhances transparency and security, fostering trust and participation in democratic processes. In welfare programs, it eliminates inefficiencies and fraud, ensuring aid reaches those who need it most.

The real-world examples from Estonia, West Virginia, and the United Nations highlight blockchain's versatility and transformative potential. By embracing this technology, governments can deliver services that are not only more efficient but also more equitable and trustworthy. These advancements set the stage for a future where public administration is more transparent, accessible, and citizen-centric.

Next, we'll explore how blockchain is shaping the global economy, expanding its impact beyond cryptocurrencies and into new territories of trade, finance, and innovation.

Part 3: Blockchain's Role in the Global Economy

Chapter 6: Cryptocurrency Beyond Bitcoin

Bitcoin's creation in 2008 sparked a revolution in digital currencies, offering a decentralized alternative to traditional money. However, as its adoption grew, significant challenges emerged. Bitcoin's volatility made it unreliable for everyday transactions, and its decentralized nature posed concerns for governments seeking to maintain control over monetary policy. In response, two transformative innovations have emerged: **Stablecoins**, which offer the stability of traditional financial systems, and **Central Bank Digital Currencies (CBDCs)**, designed to modernize economies while retaining centralized oversight. Together, these advancements represent the evolving landscape of digital currencies and their growing role in the global economy.

Stablecoins: Stability Meets Innovation

Bitcoin's value can fluctuate dramatically within hours, a trait that has limited its use as a practical medium of exchange. To address this, **stablecoins** were introduced, offering the benefits of blockchain technology while maintaining a stable value by pegging to traditional assets like the US dollar, euro, or gold. This combination of innovation and predictability has made stablecoins a cornerstone of the digital economy.

Unlike Bitcoin or other cryptocurrencies, stablecoins are designed to avoid volatility. Some are backed by fiat currencies held in reserves, while others rely on algorithms to regulate supply and demand.[6] This stability enables them to function more like traditional currencies, making them ideal for transactions, savings, and integration into the broader financial system.

One of the most prominent use cases for stablecoins is in **global payments and remittances**. Traditional cross-border transactions often involve high fees, lengthy processing times, and intermediary banks. Stablecoins eliminate these inefficiencies by enabling near-instant, low-cost transfers directly between parties. For example, migrant workers can send money to their families abroad without

---

[6] Algorithmic stablecoins maintain their stability through automated protocols that adjust the supply or demand of the token. For example, when the price rises above its target, the algorithm increases supply by issuing more tokens, and when it falls below the target, the algorithm reduces supply by buying back tokens or incentivizing holders to lock them away. A popular example of a USD-backed stablecoin is USD Coin (USDC), which is fully backed by reserves and regularly audited to ensure transparency.

incurring the steep charges associated with traditional money transfer services. This not only saves money but also expands access to financial services for underserved populations.

In **e-commerce**, stablecoins are gaining traction as a seamless payment option. Unlike Bitcoin, where price volatility may deter merchants and customers, stablecoins provide predictability. Customers can make online purchases without worrying that the value of their payment will fluctuate before the transaction is settled.

Stablecoins also play a critical role in the growing ecosystem of **Decentralized Finance (DeFi)**. On platforms like Uniswap and Aave, stablecoins serve as a reliable medium of exchange and store of value. They allow users to borrow, lend, and trade assets without intermediaries, democratizing access to financial services.

Despite their advantages, stablecoins face challenges. Governments are increasingly scrutinizing their use, fearing that they could undermine traditional banking systems. Additionally, their reliance on trusted issuers for fiat-backed reserves raises concerns about transparency and accountability. These issues highlight the need for robust regulatory frameworks to ensure that stablecoins remain secure and trustworthy.

Central Bank Digital Currencies: The Future of Money?

As stablecoins have gained prominence, governments around the world have begun exploring **Central Bank Digital Currencies (CBDCs)** to retain control over their financial systems while embracing the digital future. Unlike decentralized cryptocurrencies, CBDCs are issued and regulated by central banks, offering a digital extension of traditional fiat currencies. They combine the efficiency of blockchain technology with the stability and oversight of government-issued money.

CBDCs are designed to modernize economies by addressing inefficiencies in current payment systems. Transactions that once took days to settle can now occur instantly, reducing costs and improving financial inclusion. Additionally, CBDCs are programmable, allowing governments to create innovative monetary policies. For instance, during economic downturns, central banks could issue stimulus payments directly to digital wallets, ensuring timely and targeted relief.

Countries around the world are taking unique approaches to developing CBDCs. **China** is leading the way with its **Digital Yuan**, which has been piloted in major cities and integrated into popular platforms like WeChat Pay. This initiative not only aims to modernize China's payment infrastructure but also to reduce reliance on private financial networks, strengthening the country's financial sovereignty.

In the **European Union**, the development of the **Digital Euro** seeks to provide a secure and inclusive digital payment system for its citizens. By complementing physical cash, the Digital Euro ensures that no one is left behind in the transition to a digital economy, addressing concerns about private payment platforms dominating the market.

The **Bahamas** offers another compelling example with its **Sand Dollar**, one of the first fully operational CBDCs. Designed to serve the country's dispersed island population, the Sand Dollar facilitates secure and efficient transactions, reducing the challenges associated with physical cash in remote areas.

CBDCs also have the potential to transform **cross-border payments**, an area where inefficiencies and high costs have persisted for decades. By bypassing traditional banking intermediaries, CBDCs streamline international transactions, enabling faster and more affordable trade. This could be particularly impactful for countries with economies reliant on global commerce.

However, the rise of CBDCs is not without controversy. Their centralized nature raises concerns about privacy, as governments could potentially monitor and track individual transactions. Additionally, the cost of developing and maintaining CBDC infrastructure is significant, requiring substantial investment in technology and public education. Financial institutions, too, face disruption, as CBDCs may reduce the need for traditional banking services.

The United States and the Digital Dollar

While countries like China and the Bahamas have made significant strides in developing and implementing Central Bank Digital Currencies (CBDCs), the United States is taking a more cautious approach. The idea of a "Digital Dollar" has sparked extensive debate among policymakers, economists, and industry leaders. The U.S. Federal Reserve, the Department of the Treasury, and other key institutions are actively exploring the potential benefits and challenges of introducing a CBDC.

The Federal Reserve's Exploration of CBDCs

The Federal Reserve has acknowledged the transformative potential of a digital dollar and is conducting research to understand its implications. In 2022, the Federal Reserve released a detailed discussion paper outlining the possible design features and impacts of a CBDC. The paper emphasized key objectives for a U.S. CBDC:

- **Preserving the U.S. Dollar's Global Role**: As the world's primary reserve currency, the U.S. dollar underpins international trade and finance. A digital dollar could help maintain this dominance in an increasingly digital global economy.

- **Enhancing Payment Systems**: A CBDC could streamline domestic and cross-border payments, making transactions faster and more efficient.

- **Promoting Financial Inclusion**: By providing direct access to digital currency, the Federal Reserve aims to offer unbanked and underbanked populations a way to participate in the financial system.

However, the Federal Reserve has emphasized that it will not proceed without explicit authorization from Congress and broad public support.

Pilot Programs and Industry Collaboration

Although the United States has not officially launched a CBDC, there have been private-sector initiatives and government partnerships to test the concept. For example:

- **Project Hamilton**: A collaboration between the Federal Reserve Bank of Boston and MIT's Digital Currency Initiative, Project Hamilton explores the technical feasibility of a CBDC. Early findings focused on building a high-performance transaction system capable of processing thousands of transactions per second while maintaining privacy and security.
- **The Digital Dollar Project**: This initiative, led by the Digital Dollar Foundation and Accenture, is working to advance research and public discussion about a U.S. CBDC. The project emphasizes the need for a robust, privacy-preserving digital currency that aligns with democratic values.

Debates and Challenges

The introduction of a digital dollar has sparked debates across various sectors. Proponents argue that a CBDC could modernize the U.S. financial system, reduce costs, and strengthen the dollar's position as the global reserve currency. However, critics raise concerns about privacy, government surveillance, and the potential impact on the banking sector.

One of the most significant challenges is balancing innovation with privacy protections. Unlike cash, a digital dollar would leave a traceable record of every transaction, raising fears about financial surveillance. Policymakers are considering ways to incorporate privacy-preserving technologies while ensuring compliance with anti-money laundering (AML) and counter-terrorism financing (CTF) regulations.

Another area of concern is the potential disruption to traditional banking models. If citizens could hold digital dollars directly with the Federal Reserve, it might reduce the role of commercial banks in the financial ecosystem. This could affect lending and interest rates, prompting the need for careful design to mitigate unintended consequences.

The Road Ahead for the Digital Dollar

As the Federal Reserve continues its research and pilot programs, the future of a U.S. CBDC remains uncertain but promising. The introduction of a digital dollar would mark a significant milestone in the evolution of money, with profound implications for the domestic economy and global financial systems. While the United States is taking a deliberate approach, its actions will undoubtedly influence the trajectory of CBDC development worldwide.

Including the United States in the conversation about CBDCs highlights the global nature of this innovation and provides context for the challenges and opportunities ahead. Let me know if you'd like to refine this further!

Shaping the Future of Money

Stablecoins and CBDCs represent two distinct but complementary approaches to the future of money. Stablecoins thrive in decentralized ecosystems, offering flexibility and innovation, while CBDCs bring the reliability of government-backed currencies into the digital age. Together, these innovations are reshaping the financial landscape, providing tools to address the inefficiencies of traditional systems while expanding access to financial services.

As these digital currencies evolve, their impact on global finance will only grow. Stablecoins will continue to integrate into decentralized platforms and everyday commerce, while CBDCs will redefine how governments interact with citizens and the global economy. Both promise a future where money is more efficient, inclusive, and adaptable to the needs of a digital world.

In the next chapter, we'll explore how blockchain technology is transforming industries, focusing on its role in trade, business, and finance. The journey from revolutionizing currency to reshaping global systems is just beginning.

Chapter 7: Blockchain for Business, Trade, and Finance

The business world is evolving rapidly, and blockchain technology stands at the forefront of this transformation. By addressing inefficiencies, enhancing transparency, and reducing costs, blockchain is revolutionizing key areas such as supply chain management and decentralized finance (DeFi). These innovations are reshaping how companies and individuals interact with global markets, creating opportunities for greater efficiency and inclusion. As blockchain integrates with other emerging technologies like artificial intelligence and the Internet of Things, its potential to optimize processes and enable real-time decision-making grows exponentially. Moreover, businesses are increasingly adopting blockchain to build trust with consumers, providing verifiable data on the origins, sustainability, and authenticity of their products and services.

Supply Chain Management: Transforming Transparency and Efficiency

Supply chains are the lifeblood of global commerce, yet they have long been plagued by inefficiencies, fraud, and a lack of visibility. Blockchain technology offers a groundbreaking solution, enabling businesses to record and track goods across every stage of the supply chain with unparalleled accuracy and transparency.

At its core, blockchain creates a single, immutable ledger where every transaction and movement of goods is recorded. This means that from the moment raw materials are sourced to the delivery of the final product, all steps are documented and accessible to stakeholders. Such transparency is invaluable in industries like food production, luxury goods, and pharmaceuticals, where authenticity and traceability are critical.

For example, consider the case of **Walmart's blockchain-based food safety system**. By integrating blockchain into its supply chain, Walmart can trace the origin of contaminated food items within seconds, a process that previously took days. This swift action not only ensures consumer safety but also reduces waste and minimizes economic losses during recalls. Beyond food, this technology is being adopted in fashion to verify the authenticity of luxury items and in pharmaceuticals to prevent counterfeit drugs from entering the market.

Blockchain's decentralized nature also eliminates the need for intermediaries. This reduces the chances of fraud, speeds up processes, and cuts administrative costs. Automation of verification tasks that once required manual intervention further streamlines operations, enabling businesses to operate more efficiently and with greater accountability.

Decentralized Finance (DeFi): Redefining Financial Systems

While blockchain has transformed industries like supply chain management, its impact on finance is perhaps even more profound. **Decentralized Finance (DeFi)** is an emerging ecosystem of financial services that operates without traditional intermediaries like banks or brokers. Instead, it leverages blockchain technology to create open, programmable systems where users can lend, borrow, and trade assets directly with one another.

DeFi platforms are powered by **smart contracts**, self-executing agreements that automatically perform actions when predefined conditions are met. These platforms operate 24/7, providing financial services to anyone with internet access, regardless of geographic or economic barriers.[7]

One of the most exciting aspects of DeFi is the concept of **tokenized assets**.[8] Blockchain allows high-value assets, such as real estate, art, or even stock shares, to be divided into smaller, digital units called tokens. This democratizes access to investment opportunities that were previously out of reach for most individuals. For instance, instead of requiring millions to invest in a

---

[7] While many DeFi platforms are accessible globally, certain countries impose legal restrictions, censorship, or regulatory barriers that block or limit user access. These measures are often implemented to comply with local laws or to control financial activities within their jurisdictions.

[8] Tokenized assets refer to the process of representing physical or digital assets as blockchain-based tokens, which can be easily traded, tracked, and managed on decentralized networks. This concept is a cornerstone of blockchain's ability to democratize access to traditionally exclusive investment opportunities.

luxury property, someone can purchase a fraction of it through tokenization, enabling greater participation in global markets.

The benefits of DeFi extend beyond inclusivity. Transactions on DeFi platforms are typically faster and cheaper than traditional banking services, as they bypass the fees and delays associated with intermediaries. Furthermore, DeFi users retain full control over their assets, offering a level of autonomy that centralized institutions cannot match.

Platforms like **Uniswap**, **Aave**, and **Compound** have become leaders in the DeFi space, enabling users to trade cryptocurrencies, earn interest, and access loans without the need for traditional banks. This democratization of finance is opening new doors for individuals and businesses alike, creating a decentralized system that is more accessible, efficient, and equitable.

The Impact of Blockchain on Trade and Finance

Blockchain's influence on business, trade, and finance is reshaping industries and creating opportunities that were unimaginable just a decade ago. In **supply chain management**, blockchain ensures the traceability of goods, reduces fraud, and builds trust among consumers and businesses. In **DeFi**, it empowers individuals with tools to manage their financial lives, breaking down barriers to entry and opening up global markets.

As blockchain adoption continues to grow, its potential to revolutionize global trade and finance becomes increasingly clear. By enhancing transparency, reducing costs, and fostering greater inclusivity, blockchain is laying the foundation for a future where businesses and individuals can interact with greater efficiency and trust.

In the next chapter, we'll discuss how blockchain technology is empowering small businesses, democratizing access to capital, and driving economic growth through innovative solutions like tokenized crowdfunding. Stay tuned to discover how blockchain is leveling the playing field for entrepreneurs worldwide.

Part 4: Modern Applications of Blockchain Technology

Chapter 8: Emerging Use Cases

Blockchain technology has grown far beyond its initial use in cryptocurrencies, finding new and transformative applications across a variety of industries. Two particularly impactful areas are **Decentralized Autonomous Organizations (DAOs) and healthcare innovations**, where blockchain is redefining governance structures and improving data management and security. These emerging use cases illustrate blockchain's potential to address persistent challenges with efficiency, transparency, and security. Additionally, blockchain is fostering innovation in sectors like supply chain logistics, intellectual property protection, and renewable energy, proving its versatility and adaptability. As blockchain continues to evolve, its integration into these diverse fields not only highlights its technological capabilities but also its capacity to create tangible benefits for businesses, individuals, and society at large.

Decentralized Autonomous Organizations (DAOs): Redefining Governance

Governance systems — whether corporate, community-based, or governmental — often grapple with inefficiencies, lack of transparency, and centralized control. Blockchain offers a revolutionary solution through **Decentralized Autonomous Organizations (DAOs)**, which empower participants to collectively make decisions without relying on traditional hierarchies or centralized leadership.

What is a DAO?

A DAO operates as an organization governed by rules encoded in **smart contracts**—self-executing agreements on a blockchain. Unlike traditional organizations with boards of directors or executive teams, DAOs rely on collective decision-making, where every member has a voice proportional to their stake or contribution.

How DAOs Work

Members of a DAO hold **tokens**, which represent their voting power or stake in the organization. Proposals for action, such as funding a project or changing organizational rules, are submitted to the group. Members vote directly on these proposals, and if a proposal receives enough support, the smart contract executes it automatically. This process ensures transparency, accountability, and efficiency, as all actions are publicly recorded on the blockchain.

Applications of DAOs

DAOs have already demonstrated their potential in several areas:

- **Corporate Governance**: Shareholders in a company can use a DAO to vote transparently on major decisions, from approving budgets to electing leadership, ensuring fair representation and reducing the risk of corruption.

- **Community Projects**: DAOs enable communities to pool resources for shared goals, such as funding local initiatives or managing common assets like parks or utilities.

- **Investment Funds**: In decentralized investment DAOs, members vote on which projects or startups to back financially. This democratized approach allows individuals to participate in decisions traditionally reserved for institutional investors.

DAOs promote inclusivity and transparency, offering a model for governance that is collaborative, democratic, and resilient. As this technology matures, it has the potential to reshape decision-making across industries and communities.

Healthcare Innovations: Enhancing Privacy, Security, and Efficiency

The healthcare industry faces ongoing challenges in managing sensitive data, ensuring patient privacy, and addressing inefficiencies in operations. Blockchain's ability to securely store and share information while preserving privacy makes it a powerful tool for overcoming these hurdles.

Securing Patient Data

Patient data is one of the most sensitive types of information, yet traditional storage systems are prone to breaches and unauthorized access. Blockchain ensures that medical records are immutable and accessible only to authorized parties. Patients retain control over their data, granting or revoking access as needed, which reduces the risk of misuse.

For example, blockchain can allow a patient to share their medical history with a specialist for a consultation while keeping the information private from other parties. This system offers both security and convenience, empowering patients to manage their own health information.

Streamlining Clinical Trials

Clinical trials are critical for advancing medical research, yet they often face issues of inefficiency, data manipulation, and lack of transparency. Blockchain addresses these challenges by creating a secure record of every stage of a trial, from data collection to results analysis. This ensures that trial results are accurate, verifiable, and compliant with regulatory standards, fostering trust among researchers, regulators, and the public.

Managing Medical Records Across Providers

One of the most frustrating aspects of healthcare for both patients and providers is the lack of seamless communication between systems. Blockchain enables the sharing of medical records across healthcare networks while maintaining strict privacy protections. This leads to faster diagnoses, better-coordinated care, and improved patient outcomes.

Examples of Blockchain in Healthcare

Several initiatives around the world are already demonstrating blockchain's transformative potential in healthcare:

- **MediLedger**: This platform uses blockchain to track pharmaceutical supply chains, ensuring that counterfeit drugs are removed from circulation and improving patient safety.

- **Estonian Healthcare System**: Estonia has integrated blockchain into its national healthcare system, allowing citizens to securely access and control their health records while enabling authorized providers to deliver better care.

- **Healthereum**: This blockchain solution focuses on improving patient engagement and streamlining administrative tasks like billing and appointment management, reducing inefficiencies in care delivery.

The Path Forward for Emerging Use Cases

The examples of DAOs and healthcare innovations illustrate the vast potential of blockchain to address real-world problems in novel ways. DAOs are redefining governance by decentralizing decision-making and empowering communities, while blockchain in healthcare is revolutionizing how sensitive data is managed and shared, ensuring privacy and efficiency.

As blockchain technology continues to mature, these emerging use cases will only grow in impact and scope. From improving trust and accountability in governance to enhancing outcomes and experiences in healthcare, blockchain is laying the foundation for a more transparent, efficient, and equitable future.

In the next chapter, we will explore blockchain's role in **Web3**, the next generation of the internet, where decentralized infrastructure promises to redefine data ownership, online identity, and the creative economy.

Chapter 9: Blockchain in Web3

The internet is evolving into a new phase known as Web3, a decentralized and user-centric paradigm that challenges the centralized structures of today's Web2. Blockchain lies at the heart of this transformation, offering tools that empower individuals to regain control over their data, identities, and creative work. By replacing centralized intermediaries with transparent and secure systems, Web3 paves the way for a more equitable digital ecosystem. This chapter delves into how blockchain technology is driving the shift toward a decentralized internet, creating new opportunities for content creators, and enabling innovative applications across various sectors, from finance to entertainment.

The Transition to Decentralized Internet Infrastructure

The current iteration of the internet, Web2, is largely controlled by centralized entities such as social media platforms, cloud storage providers, and search engines. These entities act as gatekeepers, collecting and monetizing vast amounts of user data while limiting individual control. This centralization has led to recurring issues, including privacy violations, data breaches, and monopolistic practices. Web3, powered by blockchain, seeks to address these challenges by redistributing control to the users themselves.

Decentralized Storage Solutions

One of the cornerstones of Web3 is decentralized storage. Instead of relying on centralized servers owned by large corporations, data is distributed across a network of nodes. This approach ensures greater security, resilience, and accessibility.

Technologies like the **InterPlanetary File System (IPFS)** and **Filecoin** leverage blockchain to create decentralized storage networks. These platforms store data in fragments across multiple nodes, reducing reliance on any single point of failure. If one node goes offline, the data remains accessible through other nodes in the network, offering unparalleled redundancy and security.

Self-Sovereign Identity

Web3 introduces the concept of **self-sovereign identity**, a blockchain-based framework that gives individuals complete control over their digital identities. Instead of relying on third-party platforms to authenticate identity, users can store their credentials on the blockchain and share them securely when needed. This ensures privacy and eliminates the risks associated with centralized identity management systems.

For example, rather than creating separate accounts for each service, a self-sovereign identity allows users to log in securely to multiple platforms using a single blockchain-based credential. This approach reduces exposure to data breaches and puts users in charge of their personal information.

Benefits of Decentralization

Decentralization offers several key advantages:

- **Data Ownership**: Users regain ownership of their data, deciding how it is shared and monetized. This shifts the power dynamic away from centralized platforms.

- **Enhanced Security**: By distributing data across a blockchain network, Web3 minimizes the risk of large-scale breaches that are common in centralized systems.

- **Interoperability**: Blockchain-based decentralized applications (DApps) can seamlessly interact with one another, creating an ecosystem where users can move assets and data freely across platforms.

Web3 reimagines the internet as a decentralized space, one where individuals have the tools to participate actively and transparently. By reducing reliance on centralized systems, blockchain technology fosters a digital environment that prioritizes trust, privacy, and user empowerment.

Empowering Content Creators

In the Web2 era, content creators often struggle to protect their intellectual property and receive fair compensation for their work. Centralized platforms dominate the landscape, taking significant portions of revenue and limiting creators' control over their output. Blockchain technology in Web3 offers a new model that enables creators to connect directly with their audiences, ensuring fairer and more transparent interactions.

Protecting Intellectual Property

Blockchain provides a secure way for creators to establish ownership of their work. By registering creations on an immutable ledger, creators can generate a verifiable record of ownership that is accessible to anyone. This is particularly impactful in fields like digital art, music, and writing, where unauthorized copying and theft are common.

Non-Fungible Tokens (NFTs) have become a powerful tool for content creators. NFTs allow artists to tokenize their work, creating unique digital assets that can be bought, sold, and traded on blockchain platforms. Each NFT contains metadata that links it to the original creator, ensuring provenance and authenticity.

Fair Revenue Distribution

Through **smart contracts**, blockchain automates the distribution of revenue to creators. Royalties can be programmed directly into the contract, ensuring that creators are compensated every time their work is sold or used, even in secondary markets. This eliminates the need for intermediaries and reduces delays in payments.

For instance, a musician who releases a song as an NFT can receive a percentage of every resale, creating a sustainable revenue stream. Similarly, a writer can tokenize chapters of a book, allowing readers to invest in and support their work directly.

Examples of Blockchain Empowering Creators

Blockchain is already transforming how creators work across industries:

- **Music and Art**: Platforms like **Audius** and **Rarible** allow creators to monetize their music and art directly, without relying on record labels or galleries.

- **Gaming**: Blockchain-based games like **Axie Infinity** enable players to own in-game assets, creating new opportunities for creators and gamers to earn through gameplay.

- **Video Content**: Platforms like **Theta Network** reward content creators and viewers with tokens, creating a more equitable ecosystem where value is shared fairly.

By removing gatekeepers and leveraging blockchain's transparency, creators can build stronger connections with their audiences and retain full control over their intellectual property.

The Future of Web3

Blockchain technology is the driving force behind Web3, an internet that prioritizes user control and transparency. By decentralizing data storage, enabling self-sovereign identities, and empowering creators through fair revenue models, blockchain is transforming the digital landscape.

As Web3 continues to evolve, it promises to create a more equitable and inclusive internet where individuals, not corporations, hold the power. This shift has the potential to enhance privacy, security, and creativity, fostering a digital economy that benefits everyone.

In the next chapter, we will explore how blockchain is being leveraged for **social good and sustainability**, addressing some of the most pressing global challenges through innovative applications.

Chapter 10: Social Good and Sustainability

Blockchain technology is emerging as a powerful force for addressing some of humanity's most pressing challenges, from combating climate change to improving the delivery of humanitarian aid. By enhancing transparency, accountability, and efficiency, blockchain is transforming initiatives focused on social good and environmental sustainability. Its ability to securely track carbon credits, monitor supply chains, and verify the distribution of resources ensures that efforts to tackle global issues are both effective and trustworthy. As organizations and governments adopt blockchain to drive meaningful change, the technology is proving to be a critical tool in building a more equitable and sustainable future.

Environmental Initiatives: Promoting Sustainability Through Transparency

The fight against climate change and environmental degradation demands collective action and robust accountability. Blockchain's transparent and immutable ledger provides the tools necessary to ensure that sustainability efforts are both credible and effective.

Tracking Carbon Credits

Carbon credits, which allow companies to offset their greenhouse gas emissions, play a critical role in global climate strategies. However, traditional systems for managing and trading carbon credits often lack transparency, leaving room for fraud and manipulation. Blockchain offers a solution by creating a secure, tamper-proof system for recording carbon credit transactions.

For instance, companies like **IBM** and the **Energy Web Foundation** are leveraging blockchain to develop platforms where businesses can track their carbon credit usage in real-time. These systems ensure that every transaction is verified and traceable, helping organizations meet their sustainability goals while minimizing greenwashing—a practice where entities falsely claim environmental responsibility.

Promoting Transparency in Supply Chains

Sustainability in supply chains has become a key focus for companies and consumers alike. Blockchain technology allows organizations to document the environmental impact of their supply chains, providing an immutable record of how goods are produced, transported, and sold. For example, blockchain can verify whether raw materials are sourced responsibly or if production processes align with environmental standards.

This level of transparency empowers consumers to make informed decisions, rewarding companies that prioritize sustainability and holding others accountable for harmful practices.

Incentivizing Green Behavior

Blockchain platforms can be designed to reward individuals and organizations for adopting environmentally friendly behaviors. Tokens or digital incentives can be issued for actions such as recycling, reducing energy consumption, or adopting renewable energy sources. These rewards create a measurable way to encourage and sustain green practices across industries and communities.

By increasing transparency, enhancing accountability, and incentivizing positive actions, blockchain is helping to create a more sustainable future.

Humanitarian Aid: Revolutionizing Global Relief Efforts

Delivering humanitarian aid has always been fraught with challenges, from logistical inefficiencies to corruption and resource mismanagement. Blockchain technology offers an innovative approach to ensure that aid is distributed effectively and reaches those who need it most.

Building on the Syrian Refugee Program

One of the most successful examples of blockchain in humanitarian aid is the **United Nations World Food Program's (WFP)** initiative for Syrian refugees in Jordan. Using blockchain and biometric identification, such as eye scans, the program allowed refugees to purchase food directly from local markets without the need for intermediaries like banks or aid agencies.

The impact of this initiative was profound:

- Administrative costs were significantly reduced by eliminating intermediaries.
- Transparency was enhanced, ensuring that aid was distributed equitably and accounted for at every stage.
- Refugees gained direct control over their resources, fostering dignity and self-reliance.

This program not only addressed immediate needs but also laid the groundwork for scaling blockchain to other humanitarian efforts worldwide.

Addressing Global Crises

Blockchain has the potential to address a wide range of humanitarian challenges:

- **Natural Disasters**: During disasters, blockchain can track donations and ensure they are used for their intended purposes, restoring donor trust and improving accountability.
- **Refugee Resettlement**: Blockchain can provide secure digital identities for displaced populations, enabling them to

access essential services like healthcare, education, and employment.

- **Pandemic Relief**: During health crises, blockchain can facilitate efficient distribution of vaccines, medicines, and financial assistance, ensuring that resources reach underserved communities.

Future Potential

Blockchain's decentralized nature makes it uniquely suited to overcoming infrastructure challenges in remote or disaster-affected areas. As global organizations continue to explore its capabilities, blockchain could revolutionize how aid is delivered, making relief efforts faster, more transparent, and more impactful.

The Expanding Role of Blockchain in Social Good

Blockchain's applications in environmental initiatives and humanitarian aid highlight its ability to drive meaningful change beyond commerce and finance. By bringing transparency and accountability to sustainability efforts, blockchain helps combat climate change and promote environmentally responsible practices. In the realm of humanitarian aid, blockchain ensures resources are distributed efficiently and equitably, transforming the lives of vulnerable populations.

As the technology evolves, blockchain's role in addressing global challenges will only expand. Its potential to foster a more sustainable and equitable world underscores its importance as a tool for social good, paving the way for innovative solutions to some of humanity's greatest challenges.

In the next chapter, we will explore how blockchain intersects with artificial intelligence (AI) to combat misinformation and build a more trustworthy digital ecosystem.

Chapter 11: Artificial Intelligence and Combating Misinformation

In today's digital age, the spread of misinformation has become a global challenge. Deep fakes, manipulated videos, and fake images are not just tools of deception but also weapons that can undermine trust in institutions, disrupt elections, and distort reality. Blockchain technology, with its ability to provide immutable and transparent records, offers a promising solution to this problem. By leveraging the synergy between artificial intelligence (AI) and blockchains, we can create systems that combat misinformation and foster trust in digital content. Together, these technologies can establish a verifiable chain of custody for media, ensuring authenticity from creation to dissemination. As misinformation continues to evolve in sophistication, this combination of AI and blockchain is poised to play a vital role in safeguarding the truth in a rapidly changing digital landscape.

The Challenge of Authenticity

The rapid advancement of AI has enabled the creation of realistic yet entirely fabricated content. From deep fakes that mimic public figures to AI-generated images and videos that are indistinguishable from reality, the digital landscape is increasingly fraught with falsehoods.

Understanding Deep Fakes and Fake Media

- **Deep Fakes**: AI algorithms can generate realistic videos or audio clips of individuals, making it appear as though they said or did things they never did. These have been used to spread political propaganda, damage reputations, and incite social unrest.
- **Manipulated Images and Videos**: Tools for editing media have become so advanced that detecting alterations is beyond the capacity of the human eye. This has led to the proliferation of fake news and viral misinformation.

Why This Matters

- **Political Instability**: Deep fakes can influence public opinion and elections, undermining democratic processes.

- **Erosion of Trust**: The inability to verify content erodes public confidence in media, institutions, and even personal interactions.

- **Economic Impacts**: Misinformation affects industries by distorting markets, harming brands, and spreading false narratives about products or services.

The sheer volume and sophistication of AI-generated misinformation call for robust, technology-driven solutions to preserve truth and trust.

Blockchain as a Verifier

Blockchain technology's decentralized, transparent, and immutable structure makes it a powerful tool for verifying the authenticity of digital content. By recording the origins, ownership, and changes to digital files on a distributed ledger, blockchain provides an unalterable trail of evidence that ensures accountability and trust.

How Blockchain Verifies Authenticity

1. **Content Registration**: When a piece of content, such as an image, video, or document, is created, it is registered on a blockchain with a unique digital signature (hash). This hash acts as a fingerprint for the content.

2. **Immutable Records**: Blockchain ensures that the content's metadata—including creation date, creator, and any

subsequent modifications — is permanently stored. This prevents unauthorized changes.

3. **Detection of Tampering**: Any attempt to alter the content changes its hash, signaling tampering and thus invalidating its authenticity.

4. **Decentralized Validation**: No single entity controls the verification process, ensuring transparency and reducing the risk of manipulation.

By establishing an immutable record of authenticity, blockchain restores confidence in digital media and makes it harder for bad actors to spread false information.

Applications of Blockchain for Combating Misinformation

AI Content Tracking Systems

AI-generated content, while innovative, often lacks transparency about its origins. Blockchain can solve this by recording the lifecycle of such content. From creation to editing and distribution, every step can be logged on a blockchain, making the content traceable and verifiable.

Imagine a scenario where a journalist captures a video during a breaking news event. Using blockchain, the video can be registered with a timestamp and metadata about its source. If the video is edited later, these changes are recorded on the blockchain, ensuring that viewers and publishers can differentiate between the original and altered versions.

Platforms like **Truepic** are already using blockchain to verify the authenticity of digital media. Similarly, the **Content Authenticity Initiative (CAI)**, a partnership between Adobe, Twitter, and The New York Times, is developing systems that use blockchain to provide a clear chain of custody for digital content.

Decentralized Watermarking

For creators, decentralized watermarking is another revolutionary application of blockchain. By embedding ownership information directly into the blockchain, artists, photographers, and journalists can establish indisputable proof of authorship. This ensures that their work cannot be plagiarized or misused without proper credit.

For example, a digital artist might register their artwork on the blockchain with a unique identifier. If the artwork is shared online, anyone can verify its authenticity and trace it back to the original creator. This system not only protects intellectual property but also provides creators with opportunities to monetize their work directly.

Verification on Social Media

Social media platforms, where misinformation often spreads most rapidly, can integrate blockchain to verify the origins of uploaded content. Videos and images could include blockchain-verified metadata, giving users confidence that what they see is genuine.

For instance, if a deep fake video is uploaded, the absence of a blockchain record could immediately flag it as suspicious. Alternatively, content with a verifiable origin would carry a badge of authenticity, helping users distinguish truth from fabrication.

Navigating Challenges

While blockchain offers robust tools for combating misinformation, implementing these solutions at scale requires overcoming several challenges.

- **Privacy Concerns**: Blockchain's transparency must be balanced with privacy protections to ensure sensitive information is not exposed.
- **Scalability**: Social media platforms and other global systems must be able to handle billions of transactions daily, demanding advanced infrastructure.
- **Potential Misuse**: Blockchain itself must be protected from misuse, such as the false certification of malicious content.

Addressing these challenges will be crucial for blockchain to fulfill its potential as a tool for trust in the digital age.

Building a Trustworthy Digital Ecosystem

Misinformation is one of the greatest challenges of the digital age, threatening trust in institutions, media, and public discourse. Blockchain offers a transformative pathway to restore confidence by ensuring content authenticity and empowering creators. Tools like decentralized watermarking, content tracking, and social media verification are already paving the way for a more transparent digital ecosystem.

As blockchain and AI continue to evolve, their integration promises to redefine how we interact with information. Imagine an internet where every image, video, and article carries a verifiable record of its origin and history. This vision — a world where truth is the norm, not the exception — requires global collaboration, innovative solutions, and a commitment to transparency.

The convergence of AI and blockchain is more than a technical innovation; it is a critical step toward preserving truth and integrity in an increasingly complex digital landscape. By addressing misinformation at its root, these technologies hold the potential to strengthen democratic institutions, foster trust in media, and empower individuals in a rapidly changing world.

Part 5: Challenges and Future Directions

Chapter 12: Ongoing Concerns

Blockchain technology holds remarkable potential to transform industries, but several pressing challenges must be addressed for it to reach its full promise. Scalability and regulatory uncertainty remain at the forefront of these concerns. As the blockchain ecosystem expands, addressing these issues requires innovative solutions and collaborative global efforts, balancing technological advancement with practical implementation. Additionally, concerns over energy consumption in certain consensus mechanisms and the integration of blockchain with existing infrastructure further complicate its adoption. Successfully overcoming these challenges will not only unlock blockchain's transformative capabilities but also ensure its sustainability and long-term viability in a rapidly evolving digital landscape.

Scalability: The Quest for Efficiency

Scalability remains one of the most critical challenges facing blockchain. The very architecture that ensures blockchain's transparency and security also imposes limitations on transaction speeds and energy efficiency.

Understanding Scalability Challenges

At its core, blockchain operates by recording every transaction on a decentralized ledger distributed across numerous nodes. While this ensures data integrity and immutability, it also means that every node must process and store every transaction. As usage grows, the strain on networks like Bitcoin and Ethereum increases, leading to slower transaction times and higher costs.

- **Energy Consumption:**
  The Proof-of-Work (PoW) consensus mechanism, employed by early blockchains like Bitcoin, relies on miners competing to solve complex mathematical puzzles. This process demands vast computational power, resulting in energy usage comparable to entire nations. Critics argue that blockchain's environmental impact undermines its potential benefits.

- **Network Congestion:**
  Popular blockchains often experience congestion during high activity periods. This leads to delayed transactions and inflated fees, which discourage adoption for real-time applications like retail payments or remittances.

Innovative Solutions

The blockchain community has introduced several advancements to address scalability issues without compromising the core principles of decentralization and security:

1. **Transition to Proof-of-Stake (PoS):**
   Unlike PoW, PoS selects validators based on the amount of cryptocurrency they hold and are willing to "stake" as collateral. This approach significantly reduces energy consumption. Ethereum's shift to PoS with Ethereum 2.0 is a landmark achievement in this direction.

2. **Layer 2 Solutions:**
   These are secondary protocols that operate on top of existing blockchains, reducing the load on the main network.

    - **Lightning Network:** A solution for Bitcoin, it enables faster and cheaper transactions by conducting off-chain exchanges.[9]

    - **Polygon:** A Layer 2 solution for Ethereum, it supports faster processing and lower fees for decentralized applications.[10]

---

[9] Off-chain exchanges refer to transactions that occur outside the primary blockchain but are later settled on-chain. These exchanges reduce congestion and fees on the main blockchain while maintaining the overall security and transparency of the network when finalized.
[10] Layer 2 solutions are discussed a bit more in Chapter 13 under "Layer 2 Solutions for Scalability."

3. **Sharding:**
   Sharding involves dividing a blockchain into smaller, more manageable parts (shards). Each shard processes a subset of transactions, significantly increasing overall throughput.

4. **Optimized Consensus Mechanisms:**
   Emerging blockchains like Solana and Algorand are exploring alternative consensus methods that enhance efficiency and scalability while maintaining security.

These innovations signal significant progress, but achieving global scalability remains a work in progress.

Regulatory Frameworks: Navigating Uncertainty

While blockchain's decentralized nature is one of its greatest strengths, it also presents unique challenges for regulation. The global and borderless nature of blockchain applications has created a complex landscape where rules vary widely, creating uncertainty for developers, investors, and users.

The Current Regulatory Landscape

1. **Fragmented Rules:**
   Inconsistent regulations across jurisdictions hinder blockchain's growth. For example, while some countries embrace cryptocurrencies as legal tender, others impose outright bans or ambiguous policies.

2. **Consumer Protection:**
   Scams and fraud in the cryptocurrency space, coupled with the lack of safeguards, have led to significant financial losses. Governments are under pressure to create frameworks that protect users while encouraging innovation.

3. **Privacy vs. Transparency:**
   Blockchain's transparency is a double-edged sword. Public ledgers expose all transactions, potentially violating privacy laws such as GDPR. Balancing transparency with privacy is a critical challenge for policymakers.

Examples of Regulatory Approaches

Countries worldwide are adopting diverse strategies to address blockchain regulation:

- **European Union:**
  The EU's Markets in Crypto-Assets (MiCA) framework is designed to standardize rules across member states, fostering innovation while ensuring compliance.

- **United States:**
  Regulation remains fragmented, with agencies like the SEC and CFTC vying for oversight. Recent legislative proposals aim to clarify the status of cryptocurrencies and blockchain-based assets.

- **Singapore and Japan:**
  These nations lead in establishing clear, forward-thinking policies that support blockchain innovation while maintaining consumer protections.

Toward a Unified Framework

Achieving a global consensus on blockchain regulation requires collaboration among governments, international organizations, and industry stakeholders. Initiatives such as regulatory sandboxes allow for controlled experimentation with blockchain applications, paving the way for broader adoption.

Ethical Considerations in Blockchain Adoption

Beyond the technical and regulatory concerns, blockchain raises important ethical questions:

1. **Environmental Impact:**
   While solutions like PoS address energy usage, concerns remain about the carbon footprint of blockchain networks. Integrating blockchain with renewable energy sources can mitigate this impact.

2. **Inclusivity:**
   Blockchain's decentralized nature has the potential to empower underrepresented communities. However, ensuring equitable access to blockchain infrastructure and education is vital to prevent technological disparities.

3. **Potential for Misuse:**
   Blockchain's anonymity and immutability can enable illicit activities, such as money laundering or the propagation of harmful content. Policymakers must address these risks without stifling innovation.

Looking Ahead: The Road to Maturity

Looking ahead, the road to blockchain's maturity is paved with opportunities for overcoming scalability and regulatory uncertainty—challenges that, rather than deterring progress, drive innovation and collaboration. The evolution of blockchain depends on addressing these barriers while staying true to its foundational principles of decentralization, transparency, and security. Developers play a crucial role by designing scalable and energy-efficient blockchain solutions that enhance usability without compromising performance. At the same time, governments must adopt balanced approaches, fostering innovation while implementing safeguards to protect users and ensure compliance. Industry stakeholders also have a significant responsibility to collaborate in establishing interoperable and inclusive standards that create a seamless ecosystem for blockchain applications. Together, these efforts will propel blockchain technology toward its full potential, securing its place as a transformative force in the global economy.

A Vision for the Future

As these challenges are addressed, blockchain has the potential to become a cornerstone of the digital economy, enabling a world where transactions are faster, more secure, and more transparent. Whether through decentralized finance, supply chain management, or environmental sustainability, the possibilities are boundless.

Blockchain's journey is far from over, but its trajectory is clear. By tackling these ongoing concerns head-on, the technology will not only solidify its place in the global economy but also pave the way for a more equitable, efficient, and sustainable future.

Chapter 13: Innovations on the Horizon

Blockchain technology continues to evolve, with groundbreaking innovations promising to address its current limitations while unlocking new possibilities. Two key areas of advancement — Layer 2 scalability solutions and quantum-resistant security measures — are driving this evolution, shaping a future where blockchain is more efficient, secure, and scalable. These innovations not only enhance blockchain's usability for mainstream applications but also pave the way for entirely new use cases in fields like finance, healthcare, and logistics. As developers refine these technologies, blockchain's potential to integrate seamlessly with emerging fields such as AI and IoT becomes increasingly evident. This ongoing innovation ensures that blockchain remains a cornerstone of the digital economy, ready to adapt to future challenges and opportunities.

Layer 2 Solutions for Scalability

The growing adoption of blockchain has highlighted a critical challenge: scalability. Layer 2 solutions address this issue by creating secondary layers that operate on top of existing blockchains, enhancing their capacity without altering their foundational structure.

Layer 2 solutions work by handling transactions off-chain while ensuring that the main blockchain remains secure and transparent. Bundled transactions are periodically recorded on the main blockchain, combining efficiency with the trust that blockchains inherently provide. This approach significantly reduces transaction times and fees, making blockchain technology more practical for everyday use.

Key Examples of Layer 2 Solutions:

- **Lightning Network for Bitcoin**:
  The Lightning Network establishes payment channels between users, allowing multiple transactions to occur off-chain. Only the final balance is recorded on the Bitcoin blockchain. This drastically reduces fees and enhances speed, transforming Bitcoin into a viable option for microtransactions and real-time payments.

- **Polygon for Ethereum**:
  Polygon processes transactions off-chain while maintaining compatibility with Ethereum's main network. By easing congestion and lowering fees, it makes Ethereum-based applications—such as decentralized finance (DeFi), gaming, and NFTs—more accessible to a broader audience.

Impact of Layer 2 Innovations: Layer 2 solutions are pivotal in ensuring blockchain's usability at scale. Faster transaction speeds and lower fees enhance user experience, encouraging broader adoption. These advancements are particularly crucial for supporting the growth of decentralized applications (DApps), which rely on efficient, scalable networks to function effectively. As these solutions continue to mature, they will redefine blockchain's role in the digital economy, making it a viable competitor to traditional payment systems.

Quantum Computing and Security

While blockchain is renowned for its robust security, the rise of quantum computing poses a significant challenge. Unlike classical computers, quantum computers can process vast amounts of information simultaneously, potentially breaking the cryptographic algorithms that secure blockchain networks.

Risks Posed by Quantum Computing:

- **Breaking Public-Key Cryptography**:
  Current blockchain security relies on cryptographic algorithms like RSA and ECC to protect transactions and wallets. Quantum computers could potentially crack these algorithms, exposing blockchains to unauthorized access and fraud.

- **Compromising Private Keys**:
  If a quantum computer can derive private keys from public

keys, it could gain control over wallets, undermining the trust that blockchain systems depend on.[11]

To counter these risks, developers and cryptographers are already creating solutions that secure blockchain systems against potential quantum attacks.

Emerging Quantum-Resistant Solutions:

- **Post-Quantum Cryptography**:
  Algorithms such as lattice-based cryptography and hash-based signatures are being developed to withstand the computational power of quantum machines. These methods aim to protect blockchains against future threats.

- **Quantum-Resistant Blockchains**:
  Projects like Quantum Resistant Ledger (QRL) and Hyperledger are incorporating quantum-proof standards into their protocols, ensuring long-term resilience.

Proactive Adaptation:
Transitioning to quantum-resistant cryptographic standards is a proactive step to safeguard blockchain networks. While quantum computing remains in its early stages, the development of

---

[11] Private keys are critical to blockchain security, as they enable users to sign transactions and access their digital assets. If compromised, an attacker could perform unauthorized transactions, effectively taking control of a user's wallet and assets without their consent.

quantum-resilient systems ensures that blockchain remains secure, even as technology evolves.

Building a Resilient Blockchain Future

Layer 2 scalability solutions and quantum-resistant security measures represent the forefront of blockchain innovation, tackling two of the technology's most pressing challenges. By improving transaction speeds and reducing costs, Layer 2 solutions pave the way for blockchain's widespread adoption across industries. Simultaneously, the development of quantum-resistant protocols secures blockchain's foundations against the threats posed by future advancements in computing.

These innovations reflect blockchain's adaptability and resilience. As the technology continues to evolve, it is not only addressing existing limitations but also expanding its potential to transform industries, empower users, and shape the digital economy. Blockchain's future is being built today through these groundbreaking advancements, ensuring its relevance and impact for generations to come.

Chapter 14: The Future of Blockchain

Blockchain technology is poised to become a cornerstone of the digital age, shaping industries, individual experiences, and technological advancements. Its trajectory suggests a future of mass adoption across various sectors, supported by seamless integration with emerging technologies like artificial intelligence (AI), the Internet of Things (IoT), and augmented/virtual reality (AR/VR). As blockchain evolves, it promises not only to transform industries but also to redefine trust, transparency, and efficiency in a rapidly digitizing world. With applications ranging from secure identity management to decentralized marketplaces, its potential to create more equitable systems is unparalleled. By bridging gaps between traditional systems and digital innovation, blockchain is set to drive the next wave of global technological progress.

Mass Adoption Predictions

The path to blockchain's widespread adoption is already visible as it transitions from a niche innovation to a fundamental infrastructure underpinning numerous industries. By addressing longstanding inefficiencies and enhancing transparency, blockchain is set to become the backbone of many critical sectors.

Becoming the Backbone of Key Industries

Blockchain is reshaping industries by improving efficiency, security, and operational transparency.

- **Finance**: Blockchain's role in finance is transformative, streamlining payment systems and enabling decentralized finance (DeFi) platforms that remove intermediaries. Central bank digital currencies (CBDCs), powered by blockchain, are set to revolutionize monetary systems by offering faster, more secure, and cost-effective transactions.

- **Healthcare**: In healthcare, blockchain ensures the secure handling of sensitive patient records while enabling seamless data sharing among providers. It also enhances supply chain integrity for pharmaceuticals, ensuring that medications are authentic and traceable from manufacturer to patient.

- **Supply Chains**: Industries like food, fashion, and electronics are using blockchain to enhance transparency and traceability. By providing a tamper-proof record of a product's journey, blockchain reduces fraud, ensures quality control, and builds consumer trust.

Expanding Use in Identity Management

Blockchain's decentralized design is ideal for managing digital identities. Self-sovereign identity systems empower individuals to control their personal information, reducing risks of fraud and breaches. Governments and organizations are leveraging blockchain for secure digital IDs, passports, and access control systems. By granting individuals autonomy over their data, blockchain redefines privacy and security in the digital realm.

As mass adoption accelerates, blockchain will fundamentally alter how industries operate, fostering ecosystems that prioritize transparency, efficiency, and trust.

Integration with Emerging Technologies

Blockchain's transformative potential is amplified when integrated with other cutting-edge technologies. Together, these synergies promise innovations that extend far beyond blockchain's current capabilities.

Combining Blockchain with AI

AI's strength lies in analyzing vast datasets and generating insights, while blockchain excels at maintaining secure, transparent, and tamper-proof records. When combined, these technologies can address critical challenges in trust and authenticity:

- **Deep Fake Detection**: Blockchain can store immutable records of AI-generated content, making it easier to verify authenticity and combat manipulated media.
- **Secure Data Handling**: AI systems can leverage blockchain to ensure the integrity and provenance of training data, enhancing decision-making accuracy and reliability.

Internet of Things (IoT)

The IoT ecosystem, comprising interconnected devices, generates immense amounts of data that require secure and efficient management.[12] Blockchain provides the foundation for reliable communication and data sharing among devices:

- **Secure Interoperability**: Blockchain ensures that IoT devices communicate securely without centralized intermediaries.
- **Use Cases**: Applications range from smart homes to industrial IoT, where blockchain enhances security and operational reliability. For instance, connected cars can use blockchain to validate software updates or exchange data with infrastructure systems in real-time.

---

[12] The Internet of Things (IoT) ecosystem includes a vast array of devices such as smart home appliances, wearable technology, industrial sensors, and connected vehicles. These devices communicate and exchange data, creating a need for robust solutions to ensure the security and integrity of the information they generate.

Synergies with AR/VR for Metaverse Applications

Blockchain is becoming a foundational layer for the metaverse, where AR/VR technologies create immersive digital environments. In this realm, blockchain enables secure ownership and transactions, fostering trust and innovation:

- **Ownership of Digital Assets**: Blockchain ensures that users own virtual items like real estate, collectibles, and NFTs, offering secure and transparent proof of ownership.

- **Decentralized Platforms**: In the metaverse, blockchain allows users to create, trade, and monetize content without relying on centralized platforms.

- **Enhanced User Trust**: By safeguarding virtual identities and assets, blockchain supports the growth of decentralized and trustworthy digital ecosystems.

Through its integration with AI, IoT, and AR/VR, blockchain is expanding its impact, driving innovations that were once unimaginable.

Building a Blockchain-Enabled Future

The future of blockchain is not just about its technological capabilities but also its role as a transformative force across industries and daily life. As the technology becomes a backbone for sectors like finance, healthcare, and supply chains, it will create systems that are more efficient, transparent, and secure. Meanwhile, its integration with emerging technologies will redefine how we interact with digital ecosystems, ensuring trust and connectivity in an increasingly interconnected world.

The roadmap for blockchain points toward a future of limitless possibilities. Its evolution will not only address today's challenges but also lay the foundation for a new era of innovation, collaboration, and empowerment. As blockchain continues to integrate with and amplify other technologies, it will shape a digital landscape that prioritizes trust, inclusivity, and progress for generations to come.

Conclusion

Blockchain's Next Chapter

Blockchain stands as one of the most transformative innovations of the 21st century, a technology born out of necessity that has since evolved to redefine the way we think about trust, collaboration, and systems of governance. Its potential is vast, stretching across industries, economies, and borders, making it a foundation for a future where transparency, security, and efficiency are paramount. As blockchain technology matures, its integration with other emerging technologies will amplify its impact, unlocking new opportunities for innovation and collaboration. The journey ahead will require continued exploration, adaptation, and thoughtful governance to ensure blockchain fulfills its promise. Ultimately, blockchain's next chapter will be shaped by how society chooses to harness its power for a more equitable and interconnected world.

Blockchain's Enduring Promise: Trust in a Trustless World

At its heart, blockchain delivers on a simple yet profound promise: trust in a trustless world. By removing the need for intermediaries and embedding trust directly into its decentralized structure, blockchain creates systems that are inherently reliable and transparent. Every transaction, every record, and every agreement is securely stored on an immutable ledger, accessible yet tamper-proof.

This trustless architecture is more than a technical innovation—it is a response to the complexities of a digital age where trust in centralized institutions is often strained. Whether it is authenticating identities, safeguarding intellectual property, or enabling secure transactions, blockchain offers a mechanism for building confidence in the interconnected yet vulnerable systems we rely on today.

Reshaping Economies, Governments, and Global Systems

Blockchain's impact transcends its technological framework, becoming a catalyst for systemic change in economies, governance, and global collaboration.

- **Economies**: By empowering decentralized finance (DeFi), tokenized assets, and innovative ownership models, blockchain fosters inclusivity and economic participation. Entrepreneurs gain access to global markets, individuals regain control of their finances, and new value ecosystems are created.

- **Governments**: Blockchain has the potential to revolutionize public administration by streamlining processes and increasing transparency. Voting systems become more secure, public records more accessible, and services more equitable.

- **Global Systems**: On an international scale, blockchain is creating frameworks for trust and accountability in areas like supply chain management, humanitarian aid, and environmental sustainability. Its borderless nature facilitates collaboration, ensuring that global challenges are addressed with efficiency and transparency.

Blockchain's transformative power is reshaping the way we interact with systems, creating a world where efficiency, fairness, and accountability are prioritized.

Embracing Decentralized Systems

To fully realize blockchain's potential, a cultural shift toward decentralization is necessary. Traditional systems often rely on hierarchical structures and central authorities, but blockchain challenges these norms, inviting us to rethink how we share responsibility and manage trust.

Embracing decentralized systems means:

- **Fostering Transparency**: Ensuring that processes are open and verifiable to build confidence among all stakeholders.

- **Empowering Individuals**: Returning ownership of data, assets, and decisions to individuals, creating systems where people have greater control over their interactions.

- **Reinforcing Fairness**: Designing systems that reduce disparities and create opportunities for all participants.

Decentralization is not just a technical shift but a philosophical one. It invites us to build systems that reflect our values—fairness, inclusivity, and security.

A Call to Action

As blockchain moves closer to mainstream adoption, its future depends on the actions and decisions of individuals, organizations, and governments. Each of us has a role to play in shaping its trajectory.

- **Learn and Explore**: Engage with blockchain's tools, platforms, and communities. Understanding the technology is the first step to realizing its potential.

- **Advocate for Ethical Use**: Promote the responsible adoption of blockchain, ensuring that it is implemented inclusively, sustainably, and transparently. Policies should protect privacy, encourage innovation, and address inequalities.

- **Envision New Applications**: Think beyond what blockchain is currently achieving. Whether in healthcare, education, or climate action, its versatility offers endless opportunities to address pressing global challenges.

Blockchain is more than a technology—it is a tool for reimagining systems and fostering innovation that benefits everyone.

Final Thoughts

The story of blockchain is still unfolding. Its promise of trust, transparency, and efficiency lays the groundwork for a future where systems serve humanity's collective needs. Blockchain's ability to reshape economies, governments, and global systems positions it as a driving force for a more connected, equitable, and resilient world.

This chapter is both an ending and a beginning — a conclusion to a narrative about blockchain's potential and an invitation to take part in its evolution. Whether as a builder, an advocate, or a curious observer, your engagement with blockchain can help shape its future.

Together, we can navigate the challenges, embrace the opportunities, and unlock the transformative power of blockchain to create a digital era defined by trust, inclusion, and innovation.

Glossary

This glossary provides definitions for key blockchain terms used throughout the book, offering readers a quick reference for understanding important concepts and technologies.

Refer to this glossary as you explore the book to clarify terms and deepen your understanding of blockchain concepts. Each definition connects to the broader themes of transparency, security, and innovation central to blockchain technology.

51% Attack
A potential vulnerability in blockchain systems where an entity gains control of more than 50% of the network's computational power, enabling them to manipulate the blockchain.

Blockchain
A decentralized, distributed ledger that records transactions in a secure and transparent manner. Each transaction is grouped into blocks, which are linked together in chronological order to form a chain.

Blockchain Explorer
A tool that allows users to view detailed information about blockchain transactions, addresses, and blocks in a network.

Blockchain Interoperability
The ability of different blockchains to communicate and interact

with one another, enabling seamless data and asset transfer across networks.

Carbon Credits
Tradable certificates that represent the right to emit a specific amount of greenhouse gases. Blockchain enables transparent tracking and trading of carbon credits to promote sustainability.

Central Bank Digital Currency (CBDC)
A digital form of a nation's currency issued and regulated by the central bank. CBDCs aim to modernize payment systems and provide secure, government-backed alternatives to cryptocurrencies.

Consensus Algorithm
The process by which blockchain participants agree on the validity of transactions and the state of the ledger. Examples include Proof-of-Work (PoW) and Proof-of-Stake (PoS).

Consensus Mechanism
The process by which participants in a blockchain network agree on the validity of transactions. Examples include Proof-of-Work (PoW) and Proof-of-Stake (PoS).

Cryptocurrency
A digital or virtual currency that uses cryptography for security. Cryptocurrencies operate on decentralized networks and often serve as a medium of exchange within blockchain systems (e.g., Bitcoin, Ethereum).

Decentralized Application (DApp)
An application that runs on a blockchain network, leveraging its decentralized, secure, and transparent infrastructure.

Decentralized Autonomous Organization (DAO)
An organization governed by smart contracts and blockchain technology, allowing members to participate in decision-making through decentralized voting without centralized leadership.

Decentralized Exchange (DEX)
A peer-to-peer marketplace that allows users to trade cryptocurrencies directly without relying on centralized intermediaries.

Decentralized Finance (DeFi)
A financial ecosystem built on blockchain technology that enables peer-to-peer transactions without intermediaries like banks. DeFi includes services like lending, borrowing, and trading through decentralized applications (DApps).

Digital Identity
A blockchain-based system for managing personal identity information, allowing individuals to control access to their data securely and transparently.

Distributed Ledger
A digital ledger that is shared, replicated, and synchronized across multiple nodes in a blockchain network. All participants have access to an identical copy of the ledger.

Fork
A change to the blockchain protocol that can result in a split, creating two separate versions of the blockchain. Forks can be soft (backward-compatible) or hard (not backward-compatible).

Gas Fees
Transaction fees paid by users to process and validate operations

on a blockchain network. Common in networks like Ethereum, gas fees incentivize miners or validators to secure the network.

Governance Token
A token that gives holders the right to vote on decisions affecting a blockchain network or decentralized organization.

Hash
A unique alphanumeric code generated by a mathematical function to represent data. Hashing ensures the integrity of data on a blockchain, as even a small change in the data will produce a completely different hash.

Immutable
A key characteristic of blockchain, meaning data cannot be altered or deleted once it has been recorded.

Initial Coin Offering (ICO)
A fundraising method in which blockchain-based projects sell tokens to investors in exchange for funding. ICOs are often used by startups in the cryptocurrency space.

Interoperability
The ability of different blockchain networks to communicate and share data. Interoperability enhances the functionality and adoption of blockchain systems.

Layer 2 Solutions
Technologies built on top of existing blockchains to improve scalability, reduce transaction costs, and increase efficiency. Examples include the Lightning Network (Bitcoin) and Polygon (Ethereum).

Merkle Tree
A data structure used in blockchain to efficiently verify large

amounts of data. It organizes transaction data into a hierarchical tree format, improving security and speed.

Mining
The process of validating transactions and adding new blocks to a blockchain. Miners compete to solve complex mathematical puzzles, earning rewards in the form of cryptocurrency.

Node
A computer that participates in a blockchain network by storing a copy of the blockchain ledger and validating transactions.

Non-Fungible Token (NFT)
A unique digital asset that represents ownership of a specific item, such as art, music, or virtual property. Unlike cryptocurrencies, NFTs are not interchangeable.

Private Key
A secret code used to sign transactions and prove ownership of blockchain assets. Private keys must be kept secure to prevent unauthorized access to funds or data.

Proof-of-Stake (PoS)
A consensus mechanism in which validators secure the blockchain by staking cryptocurrency. PoS is more energy-efficient than Proof-of-Work (PoW).

Proof-of-Work (PoW)
A consensus mechanism that requires network participants to solve complex mathematical problems to validate transactions and create new blocks. PoW is used by Bitcoin and other early blockchains.

Public Key
A cryptographic code derived from a private key that is shared

publicly. It allows others to send assets or data to a blockchain wallet.

Quantum-Resistant Cryptography
Advanced cryptographic techniques designed to withstand the computational power of quantum computers, ensuring the long-term security of blockchain systems.

Smart Contract
A self-executing contract with terms encoded directly into code on a blockchain. Smart contracts automatically execute actions when predefined conditions are met.

Smart Token
A programmable token that can execute specific actions or represent conditional ownership using smart contracts.

Stablecoin
A cryptocurrency pegged to a stable asset like the US dollar, designed to minimize price volatility.

Staking
The process of locking cryptocurrency in a blockchain network to participate in validation or governance and earn rewards.

Token
A digital asset built on an existing blockchain, often representing ownership, utility, or governance rights in a project or platform.

Tokenization
The process of converting rights or assets into digital tokens that can be traded or transferred on a blockchain. Examples include tokenized real estate or digital art.

Tokenomics

The economic model of a cryptocurrency or token, detailing how it is distributed, used, and managed within a blockchain ecosystem.

Wallet

A digital tool that stores private and public keys, allowing users to send, receive, and manage cryptocurrencies or digital assets.

Web3

The next generation of the internet characterized by decentralization and user empowerment. Web3 uses blockchain to give individuals control over their data and digital identities.

Key Takeaways

This section provides a concise summary of the key points covered in each chapter, offering a quick reference to the core concepts and ideas presented in the book.

Part 1: Foundations of Blockchain Technology

Chapter 1: Origins and Evolution

- Blockchain originated in 2008 as the foundation for Bitcoin, solving the problem of trustless digital transactions.
- Its evolution beyond cryptocurrency has opened doors to applications in smart contracts, NFTs, and decentralized finance (DeFi).
- Blockchain's role in today's economy is foundational, addressing trust, efficiency, and security challenges across industries.

Chapter 2: What is Blockchain?

- Blockchain is a decentralized, immutable ledger ensuring transparency and security in transactions.
- Key features include decentralization, transparency, and advanced cryptographic security, making it adaptable to diverse applications.

- Its structure ensures trust by design, eliminating intermediaries.

Chapter 3: How Blockchain Has Evolved

- Blockchain has progressed from its use in digital currencies to enabling complex applications like smart contracts, NFTs, and DeFi.

- Innovations such as Ethereum's programmability have transformed blockchain into a versatile platform for digital ecosystems.

- New use cases showcase blockchain's ability to revolutionize ownership, governance, and financial systems.

Part 2: Blockchain in Governance

Chapter 4: Governments and Blockchain

- Governments are leveraging blockchain for secure record-keeping, digital identities, and land registries.

- Case studies from Estonia, Illinois, and Dubai illustrate blockchain's potential in public administration.

- Challenges include regulatory hurdles, balancing transparency with privacy, and addressing technical literacy gaps.

Chapter 5: Blockchain for Public Services

- Blockchain enhances voting systems with transparency and tamper-proof mechanisms, strengthening democratic processes.

- In welfare programs, blockchain ensures aid distribution reaches intended recipients while reducing fraud.

- The UN's blockchain program for Syrian refugees demonstrates blockchain's potential to revolutionize humanitarian efforts.

Part 3: Blockchain's Role in the Global Economy

Chapter 6: Cryptocurrency Beyond Bitcoin

- Stablecoins address volatility, making cryptocurrencies practical for everyday use and global remittances.

- Central Bank Digital Currencies (CBDCs) represent governments' modernization of financial systems, with projects like China's digital yuan and the EU's digital euro leading the way.

- Blockchain is reshaping the global financial system, providing secure and inclusive solutions.

Chapter 7: Blockchain for Business, Trade, and Finance

- In supply chains, blockchain enhances transparency, traceability, and efficiency, as seen in Walmart's food safety initiative.

- Decentralized finance (DeFi) eliminates intermediaries, enabling peer-to-peer lending, borrowing, and trading.
- Tokenized assets democratize ownership, allowing fractional investments in real estate, art, and other high-value assets.

Part 4: Modern Applications of Blockchain Technology

Chapter 8: Emerging Use Cases

- Decentralized Autonomous Organizations (DAOs) redefine governance through collective, transparent decision-making.
- In healthcare, blockchain secures patient data, streamlines clinical trials, and enhances the privacy of medical records.
- Emerging applications illustrate blockchain's versatility in addressing industry-specific challenges.

Chapter 9: Blockchain in Web3

- Web3's decentralized infrastructure shifts data ownership to individuals, fostering trust and reducing reliance on centralized platforms.
- Blockchain empowers content creators with tools to protect intellectual property and ensures fair revenue distribution.
- Integration with decentralized applications (DApps) is creating new digital ecosystems.

Chapter 10: Social Good and Sustainability

- Blockchain promotes sustainability by tracking carbon credits and creating transparency in environmental efforts.

- Humanitarian initiatives, like the UN's Syrian refugee program, leverage blockchain to enhance aid distribution and accountability.

- These use cases demonstrate blockchain's ability to drive social good and global sustainability.

Chapter 11: Artificial Intelligence and Blockchain

- Blockchain addresses the challenge of authenticity in AI-generated content by creating immutable records and decentralized watermarking.

- Integration of AI and blockchain combats misinformation, enhancing trust in digital content.

- Blockchain's transparency supports ethical AI applications and ensures content accountability.

Part 5: Challenges and Future Directions

Chapter 12: Ongoing Concerns

- Scalability issues are being addressed through innovations like Layer 2 solutions and energy-efficient consensus mechanisms.

- Regulatory challenges require international collaboration and balanced frameworks to foster innovation while protecting users.

- The ongoing evolution of blockchain is both a challenge and an opportunity to strengthen its global impact.

Chapter 13: Innovations on the Horizon

- Layer 2 solutions, such as the Lightning Network and Polygon, improve scalability, reducing costs and increasing efficiency.
- Quantum-resistant cryptographic solutions are emerging to safeguard blockchain against future threats from quantum computing.
- These innovations are ensuring blockchain's resilience and adaptability for future applications.

Chapter 14: The Future of Blockchain

- Blockchain is becoming foundational for industries such as finance, healthcare, and supply chains.
- Integration with emerging technologies like AI, IoT, and AR/VR is unlocking new possibilities and driving innovation.
- Blockchain's decentralized and secure architecture is creating a more equitable, transparent, and efficient digital ecosystem.

Chapter 15: Blockchain's Next Chapter

- Blockchain's promise lies in its ability to create trust in a decentralized world.
- Embracing blockchain requires a mindset shift toward decentralization, empowering individuals and fostering transparency and collaboration.

More Reading and Learning

Resources for Further Reading and Learning

To deepen your understanding of blockchain technology and explore its many applications, the following resources offer valuable insights, practical knowledge, and industry updates. Whether you are new to blockchain or looking to expand your expertise, these materials provide a solid foundation for further learning.

Books

1. **"Blockchain Basics: A Non-Technical Introduction in 25 Steps" by Daniel Drescher**
   A beginner-friendly guide that explains blockchain concepts in a step-by-step approach.

2. **"Mastering Bitcoin: Unlocking Digital Cryptocurrencies" by Andreas M. Antonopoulos**
   A comprehensive resource for understanding Bitcoin and blockchain technology, suitable for both technical and non-technical readers.

3. **"The Basics of Bitcoins and Blockchains" by Antony Lewis**
   Covers blockchain fundamentals, cryptocurrency concepts, and real-world applications.

4. **"Blockchain Revolution" by Don Tapscott and Alex Tapscott**
   Explores how blockchain is transforming industries and societies.

Online Courses

1. **"Blockchain Basics" by the University at Buffalo (Coursera)**
   A free, beginner-level course that introduces blockchain technology and its applications.

2. **"Ethereum and Solidity: The Complete Developer's Guide" (Udemy)**
   Learn how to build decentralized applications (DApps) and smart contracts on the Ethereum blockchain.

3. **"Blockchain Specialization" by the University of Nicosia (Coursera)**
   A multi-course program covering blockchain fundamentals, cryptocurrencies, and smart contracts.

4. **"MIT Media Lab: Blockchain and Money" (OpenCourseWare)**
   A lecture series exploring blockchain's role in the economy, offered by MIT.

Websites and Blogs

1. **CoinDesk.com**
   A leading source for blockchain news, industry trends, and in-depth analysis.

2. **Blockchain.com Blog**
   Offers practical guides and updates on blockchain developments.

3. **Ethereum.org**
   The official website for Ethereum, featuring resources for developers and learners.

4. **IBM Blockchain Blog**
   Focuses on enterprise blockchain applications and case studies.

Podcasts

1. **"Unchained" with Laura Shin**
   Explores blockchain, cryptocurrency, and DeFi topics with expert guests.

2. **"The Bad Crypto Podcast"**
   A lighthearted yet informative look at blockchain technology and cryptocurrency trends.

3. **"The Blockchain Show"**
   Covers blockchain developments, use cases, and future possibilities.

Research Papers and Whitepapers

1. **"Bitcoin: A Peer-to-Peer Electronic Cash System" by Satoshi Nakamoto**
   The foundational whitepaper that introduced blockchain technology.
   Read Here → https://bitcoin.org/bitcoin.pdf

2. **Ethereum Whitepaper**
   Explains the concept of smart contracts and decentralized applications.
   Read Here → https://ethereum.org/en/whitepaper/

3. **MIT Technology Review Blockchain Reports**
   In-depth articles and research on the impact of blockchain across various sectors.
   https://www.technologyreview.com/topic/blockchain/

Communities and Forums

1. **Reddit: r/Blockchain**
   A community for blockchain enthusiasts to discuss news, trends, and technical concepts.

2. **GitHub**
   Explore open-source blockchain projects and contribute to development efforts.
   https://github.com/topics/blockchain

3. **LinkedIn Groups**
   Join professional groups like "Blockchain Professionals" for

networking and discussions.
https://www.linkedin.com/company/blockchain-professionals-community/

Industry Certifications

1. **Certified Blockchain Professional (CBP)**
   A certification program for individuals seeking in-depth blockchain expertise.

2. **Certified Ethereum Developer (CED)**
   Focused on developing smart contracts and decentralized applications.

3. **Blockchain for Business (IBM)**
   A certification course emphasizing enterprise applications of blockchain.

This curated list provides a starting point for further exploration of blockchain technology. Whether you prefer books, courses, or community engagement, these resources can help you expand your knowledge and stay ahead in the rapidly evolving world of blockchain.

More References and Sources

Al Goni, N., Saad, S., & Ibrahim, A. (2020). A P2P optimistic fair-exchange (OFE) scheme for personal health records using blockchain technology. *Proceedings of the 3rd International Conference on Wireless, Intelligent, and Distributed Environment for Communication.*

Allen, H. J. (2017). $=€=Bitcoin? *Maryland Law Review*, 877-939. Retrieved from Maryland Law Review: http://www.law.umaryland.edu/academics/journals/mdlr/

Casey, M. J., & & Vigna, P. (2018). In blockchain we trust. *MIT Technology Review*.

Catalini, C. (2018). Blockchain technology and cryptocurrencies: implications for the digital economy, cybersecurity, and government. *Georgetown Journal of International Affairs*.

Del Castillo, M. (2019). *Blockchain goes to work.* Retrieved from Forbes: http://www.forbes.com/forbes/

Fenwick, M., & Vermeulen, E. (2021). *Technology and corporate governance: Blockchain, crypto, and decentralized autonomous organizations.* Retrieved from ECGI Working Paper Series in Law: https://www.ecgi.global/sites/default/files/working_papers/documents/finalfenwickvermeulen1.pdf

Hempel, J. (2018). *Wired.* Retrieved from How refugees are helping create blockchain's brand new world: https://www.wired.com/story/refugees-but-on-the-blockchain/

Kilheffer, B. A. (2019). 21st Century Blockchain Governments and Economies. *Baltimore Technology News.*

Mirkovic, J. (2017). *Blockchain Cook County: distributed ledgers for land records.* Retrieved from The Illinois Blockchain Initiative: https://illinoisblockchain.tech/blockchain-cook-county-final-report-1f56ab3bf89

Stone, A. (2015). *Unchaining innovation.* Retrieved from Government Technology: http://www.govtech.com/

The role of blockchain in a digital-first economy. (2022). Retrieved from IEEE: https://innovate.ieee.org/wp-content/uploads/2022/05/River-Blockchain.pdf

U.S. Department of Homeland Security. (n.d.). Retrieved from Blockchain portfolio. Science and Technology Directorate: https://www.dhs.gov/science-and-technology/blockchain-portfolio

Walch, A. (2018). Blockchain applications to international affairs: reasons for skepticism. *Georgetown Journal of International Affairs.*

Zaharchuk, D. (2022). *Four ways blockchain could aid governments.* Retrieved from IBM THINK: https://www.ibm.com/blogs/think/2017/01/four-ways-for-blockchain/

www.ingramcontent.com/pod-product-compliance
Lightning Source LLC
Chambersburg PA
CBHW071025240526
45469CB00006BD/2093